CATHOLIC SOCIAL
TEACHING

Fourth Revised and Expanded Edition

CATHOLIC SOCIAL TEACHING

Our Best Kept Secret

Edward P. DeBerri
James E. Hug

with
Peter J. Henriot
and Michael J. Schultheis

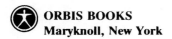

ORBIS BOOKS
Maryknoll, New York

CENTER OF CONCERN
Washington, D.C. 20017

Founded in 1970, Orbis Books endeavors to publish works that enlighten the mind, nourish the spirit, and challenge the conscience. The publishing arm of the Maryknoll Fathers & Brothers, Orbis seeks to explore the global dimensions of the Christian faith and mission, to invite dialogue with diverse cultures and religious traditions, and to serve the cause of reconciliation and peace. The books published reflect the views of their authors and do not represent the official position of the Maryknoll Society. To learn more about Maryknoll and Orbis Books, please visit our website at www.maryknoll.org.

The Center of Concern is an independent, interdisciplinary team engaged in social analysis, theological reflection, policy advocacy, and popular education on issues of social and economic justice. Founded in 1971, the Center has a long tradition of research and education on issues from a Catholic social teaching perspective. Rooted in a faith commitment and guided by a global vision, our current programs focus on international development, corporate accountability, peace initiatives, world food security, alternatives to international financial institution policies, gender and trade issues, and social theology. The Center is a non-governmental organization (NGO) holding consultative status with the United Nations. Our team engages in an extensive program of advocacy and writing to help North Americans and others around the world understand and respond to the changing global scene. A newsletter, CENTER FOCUS, is published quarterly. The Center is tax-exempt and is supported largely by donations from friends. See more about our current projects at www.coc.org. In addition, the Center provides educators and parish ministry leaders high quality ready-to-use education materials through our Education for Justice web site www.educationforjustice.org.

First U.S. edition of *Our Best Kept Secret: The Rich Heritage of Catholic Social Teaching* © 1985 by the Center of Concern, Washington, D.C. 20017

Revised and enlarged edition of *Our Best Kept Secret* © 1987 by the Center of Concern

Second revised edition, *Catholic Social Teaching: Our Best Kept Secret* © 1988 by Orbis Books and the Center of Concern

Third revised and enlarged edition © 1992 by Orbis Books, Maryknoll, NY 10545, and the Center of Concern, Washington, D.C. 20017

This present work is the fourth revised and expanded edition © 2003 by Orbis Books and the Center of Concern

Manufactured in the United States of America.

Library of Congress Cataloging-in-Publication Data

DeBerri, Edward P.
    Catholic social teaching : our best kept secret.— 4th rev. and expanded ed. / Edward P. Deberri, James E. Hug, with Peter J. Henriot and Michael J. Schultheis.
        p. cm.
    Rev. and expanded ed. of: Catholic social teaching / Peter J. Henriot, Edward P Deberri, Michael J. Schultheis. c1992.
    Includes bibliographical references
    ISBN 1-57075-485-3 (pbk.)
    1. Sociology, Christian (Catholic) 2. Catholic Church—Doctrines. I. Hug, James E. II. Henriot, Peter J. Catholic social teaching. III. Title.

BX1753.H46 2003
261.8'088'22—dc21

                                        2003049878

We dedicate this book to the hard-working educators and front-line activists who embody the principles of Catholic social teaching each day.

CONTENTS

PREFACE

The longing for justice has always been a central element in the major faith traditions. In the Judeo-Christian tradition, it has been a strong and central theme from earliest biblical times to the present. Without work for justice, declared the 1971 Synod of Catholic bishops, we do not have true Gospel living. The opening lines of *The Church in the Modern World (Gaudium et Spes)* of the Second Vatican Council stated the centrality of justice to the Christian calling most vividly:

> The joys and hopes, the sorrows and anxieties of the women and men of this age, especially those who are poor or in any way oppressed, these are the joys and hopes, the sorrows and anxieties of the followers of Christ.

The modern expression of the church's social teaching began more than a century ago with the encyclical of Pope Leo XIII, *On the Condition of Labor (Rerum Novarum)*. From this modest beginning, Catholic social teaching has grown and expanded rapidly, as you will see in the pages of this book. It represents a rising crescendo of social consciousness and concern in the church as we enter the twenty-first century.

Catholic social teaching is an effort to spell out just what it means to take up "the joys and hopes, the sorrows and anxieties" of our sisters and brothers all around the planet today. This body of principles, guidelines, and applications has developed in a rich fashion. It provides a compelling challenge for responsible Christian living today.

In 1984, in order to make this teaching more widely known, the Center of Concern prepared a small "primer" to introduce the background and key lessons of Catholic social teaching. The immediate and widespread popularity of *Our Best Kept Secret* encouraged us to revise and enlarge the original version. As the teaching has continued to develop, our revisions have multiplied. This volume is the fourth revised and enlarged edition of the work as co-published by Orbis Books and the Center of Concern.

This edition builds most immediately upon the Centenary Edition of 1992, adding treatments of Pope John Paul II's encyclical *The Gospel of*

xi

Life (Evangelium Vitae) and passages from *The Catechism of the Catholic Church* that pull together the main themes of Catholic social teaching. In a newly developed section of the book, we have added important teaching documents of regional churches. As careful local discernment of the signs of the times, they form the cutting edge of the Church's developing social vision. Because of the insights they provide into the application of Catholic social teaching, these documents deserve attention from the Church outside their local areas.

The introductory material in Part One has been revised and expanded to include comments on the new documents outlined elsewhere in the book. The section on the Major Lessons of Catholic Social Teaching has received the most extensive re-writing. It now builds upon the widely disseminated list of "Seven Key Themes of Catholic Social Teaching" published by the U.S. Conference of Catholic Bishops. Under each of those themes, it sketches more specific principles from the Catholic social tradition that are important for evaluating contemporary issues. Finally, a short fifth chapter has been added to Part One of the book, laying out some of the future challenges Catholic social teaching must face and indicating some of the directions in which it needs to move.

In Part Two and Part Three, the paragraph number citations in the outlines facilitate reference to the original documents, providing precise guidance for further exploration of the teaching. The discussion questions in Part Four have been revised and the annotated Bibliography has been updated.

The original version of *Catholic Social Teaching: Our Best Kept Secret* was prepared for use by the Church in Africa and has been reprinted several times there. The subsequent U.S. versions (1985, 1987, 1988 and 1992) circulated tens of thousands of copies and were translated and published in Europe, Asia, and Latin America.

Our gratitude for most of the document outlines, in this edition as in previous editions, is owed to Ed DeBerri. The original idea for such a volume was his. His professionalism and the high quality of his work contribute greatly to the value of this resource.

Thanks too go to Philip Berryman who provided the summary of the Portuguese text of the Brazilian bishops' document, Maria Riley, O.P., who consulted on the material discussing future directions for Catholic social thought, and the Center's Education for Justice team of Jane Deren and Maura Kristof who reviewed and revised the Study Guides in Part Four.

The Center also acknowledges our debt to Michael Schultheis, S.J., Peter Henriot, S.J., Philip Land, S.J., Simon Smith, S.J., Ken Loftus, S.J., Anne Hope, Maurice Monette, Ruth Coyne, Cindy Fowler, Lucien Chauvin, and David Simmons for their assistance with earlier versions of this book.

The Center of Concern is pleased once again to collaborate with the fine staff of Orbis Books in publishing *Catholic Social Teaching: Our Best Kept Secret*. Their hard work, courage, and dedication through the years have contributed inestimably to the church's mission of justice. Our collaboration with Robert Ellsberg and Susan Perry, our editor at Orbis Books, has been a joy.

Finally, this revised edition would not have seen the light of day except for the dedicated, sometimes unrelenting, always gracious work and encouragement of Candy Warner, the Center's Director of Administration, Communications and Finance. Candy's outstanding project management and organizational skills have been invaluable.

In November, 1986, the U.S. Catholic bishops released the final version of their major pastoral letter entitled *Economic Justice for All: Catholic Social Teaching and the U.S. Economy.* The bishops expressly call for "renewed emphasis" on Catholic social teaching in all our educational institutions, and express their hope that "through our continual reflection . . . we will be able to help refine Catholic social teaching and contribute to its further development" (#360). In 1998, the bishops evaluated their efforts and concluded that there is much more to be done to share the church's social mission and message *(Sharing Catholic Social Teaching: Challenges and Directions).*

The Center of Concern feels a deep sense of urgency to spread the knowledge of this mission and this great teaching tradition as well as to facilitate its application to the struggles and challenges of the globalizing world. The Education for Justice Network www.educationforjustice.org is one important part of the Center's response; this volume is another. It is our sincere prayer at the Center of Concern that *Catholic Social Teaching: Our Best Kept Secret* will continue to assist the Christian community, in the United States and throughout the world, to engage more effectively in the linking of faith and justice through an increased knowledge, appreciation, and implementation of the principles and vision of Catholic social teaching.

JAMES E. HUG, S.J.
Center of Concern
Washington, D.C.
March 3, 2003

PART ONE

HISTORICAL BACKGROUND

1

Our Best Kept Secret

"The best kept secret in the Roman Catholic Church in the United States!" That is how the Church's social teaching has frequently been described. *That* the Church has a developed body of teaching on social, economic, political, and cultural matters and *what* that body says seem to have been forgotten—or have never been known—by a majority of the Roman Catholic community in the United States. Even the recent commemorations of the one hundredth anniversary of the beginning of modern Catholic social teaching did not receive sustained attention in the secular or Catholic media. Catholic social teaching still remains outside the mainstream of ordinary parish life.

At least it would seem that all too few Catholics know about the Church's social teaching if we are to judge from the reactions of many U.S. Catholics to their Bishops' Peace Pastoral of 1983 and Economics Pastoral of 1986. These two important letters of the National Conference of Catholic Bishops (NCCB) have been called "radical" and criticized for not being authentically Catholic. Yet both draw heavily for their inspiration and direction upon the documents authored in recent decades by Popes, the Second Vatican Council, the Synods of Bishops, and national conferences of Bishops.

The traditional roots of the U.S. Bishops' messages can be readily noted:

The Challenge of Peace: God's Promise and Our Response examines the morality of war and peace and questions the arms race from the perspectives presented by Pope John XXIII in his encyclical *Peace on Earth* (1963), and by the statement *The Church in the Modern World* (1965) of Vatican II.

Economic Justice for All: Catholic Social Teaching and the U.S. Economy addresses such issues as unemployment, international trade, welfare policy, and governmental planning with perspectives raised in

Pope Paul VI's *Development of People* (1967), the Synod of Bishops' *Justice in the World* (1971), and Pope John Paul II's *On Human Work* (1981).

Not to know the foundation and background of these pastoral letters is to be seriously hampered in understanding their message and responding to their call.

In the not too distant past, courses in the social encyclicals were routinely offered in colleges and seminaries. Many adult education programs—such as labor schools—provided intense study of their teachings and applications. Popular handbooks explained the significance of the messages to a wide audience. But this has not been the case in recent years. The ordinary Catholic probably has heard very few homilies in her or his local parish on the topic of the social teachings.

Why is this so? Why are we keeping the social teachings "secret"? Many factors seem to have contributed to this unfortunate situation.

1. The documents usually seem to be rather abstract, dry in content, and not very attractive to pick up and read.
2. The topics frequently are quite challenging, dealing as they do with controversial social issues, and therefore they may disturb readers and make them uncomfortable.
3. A "papal encyclical" is, at least in many people's minds, almost immediately associated with *On Human Life (Humanae Vitae, 1968)* and all the debates, disputes, and dissent over the Church's position on birth control.
4. In general, authoritative statements—whether from Church or government—have less attraction today than acts of authentic witness.

But it is noteworthy that recently there has been a small resurgence of interest in the social teachings. The topic of what the Church has to say on the political and economic issues of the day is gaining new attention in ever wider circles. Courses that extensively cover Catholic social teaching are being offered in more Catholic high schools, universities, seminaries, and adult education programs. It is true that the controversial nature of some of these issues leads to many lively political debates. But it also reveals a much deeper longing on the part of Catholics and others, in response to the needs of the day.

The serious crises we face in the social order, nationally and internationally, have challenged Catholics as parents, citizens, teachers, workers, business and professional people, politicians, etc. We are looking around for explanations and guidelines which give us a Christian perspective on the contemporary social events and issues confronting our nation. What can we say, as Christians, about peace and the arms race, economic justice, international development, racism and sexism, human rights, the dignity of all persons and the sacredness of human life, work and labor unions, etc.?

More and more people are rediscovering—or discovering for the first time—the rich heritage of the Church's social teachings. We are responding with enthusiasm and sometimes with astonishment: "I didn't know there were so many good things in the encyclicals!"

Easy answers to hard problems cannot be found in the social teachings. We must resist the temptation to look for clear solutions. But what can be found is a *social wisdom* based on:

— biblical insights,
— the tradition of the early writers of the Church,
— scholastic and other Christian philosophies,
— theological reflection,
— and the contemporary experience of the People of God struggling to live out faith in justice.

What we offer in this small book is by no means a thorough presentation of the Church's social teaching as it is relevant to the United States. Rather, by way simply of an *introduction,* we aim to:

1. Provide an overview of historical development of the teaching.
2. Note the major thrust of the teaching as it has been applied to the issues of the day.
3. Show its use in documents of the Church in the United States and in the Third World.
4. Stimulate further study and reflection.

The *summaries* of the documents are intended to open up the principal elements of the teaching in an easy-to-grasp outline form. Readers are encouraged to use these summaries in conjunction with the full text of the documents themselves and to relate the documents to their historical contexts. This is essential if one is to appreciate the ongoing and dynamic relationship of the Church to a complex and changing world.

It is obvious, of course, that "introductions" and "summaries" are no substitute for actually reading, studying, and praying over the texts themselves. Then applications must be made to the real life situations of social, economic, political, and cultural conditions in the United States and around the world. This is the way to make the faith message of these documents come alive in the institutions and values of our day.

The aim of this book is *commitment.* Commitment to a faith that does justice. For since the Second Vatican Council we in the Church have come to understand more fully and appreciate more deeply that a "living faith" leads directly to a "loving action" in the transformation of the world.

2

AN EVOLVING SOCIAL MESSAGE

FROM POPE LEO XIII TO THE SECOND VATICAN COUNCIL

Reconstructing the Social Order

The Church's social teaching in the modern period dates from 1891, when Pope Leo XIII in the encyclical letter, *On the Condition of Labor (Rerum Novarum),* spoke out against the inhuman conditions which were the normal plight of working people in industrial societies. He recognized that the three key factors underlying economic life are workers, productive property, and the state. He also indicated that their just and equitable inter-relationship is the crucial issue of Catholic social teaching. Because of the principles which he set forth to guide in the formation of a just society, this document has become known as the *Magna Carta* for a humane economic and social order.

In 1931, on the occasion of the fortieth anniversary of *On the Condition of Labor,* Pope Pius XI composed the next major social encyclical, *The Reconstruction of the Social Order (Quadragesimo Anno).* Writing in the midst of a severe, world-wide economic depression, Pius XI addressed the issue of social injustice and called for the reconstruction of the social order along the lines originally set forth by Leo XIII. He reaffirmed the right and the duty of the Church to address social issues.

While condemning capitalism and unregulated competition, Pius XI also condemned communism for its promotion of class struggle and the narrow reliance for leadership on the working class (the so-called "dictatorship of the proletariat"). He stressed the social responsibilities of private property and the rights of working people to a job, to a just wage, and to organize to claim their rights. He also pointed out the positive role of governments in promoting the economic good of all people in society. Economic undertakings should be governed by justice and charity as the principal laws of social life.

During World War II, Pope Pius XII delivered several important "Christmas Messages" in which he outlined the just international order necessary for global peace. He encouraged the cooperation which resulted in the institution of the United Nations. His vision accounts for the long-standing commitment of strong support given to the United Nations by the Church's social teaching.

Thirty years after Pius XI's great letter, Pope John XXIII wrote two major social encyclical letters on the central issues of his day. In *Christianity and Social Progress* (*Mater et Magistra*, 1961) and *Peace on Earth* (*Pacem in Terris*, 1963), Pope John set forth a number of principles to guide both Christians and policy makers in addressing the gap between rich and poor nations and the threats to world peace. He called on committed Christians and "all people of good will" to work together to create local, national, and global institutions which would both respect human dignity and promote justice and peace. He emphasized that the growing interdependence among nations in a world community called for an effective world government which would look to the rights of the individual human person and promote the universal common good.

A major contribution of John XXIII was his emphasis in *Peace on Earth* on social and economic rights and not just on legal and political rights. Among the economic rights were the right to work and the right to a just wage. Reflecting the development of the United Nations' *Universal Declaration of Human Rights* (1948), this promotion of economic rights finds strong reaffirmation in the U.S. Bishops' Economics Pastoral.

The Coming of a "World" Church

When Pope John XXIII convened the Second Vatican Council in October 1962, he opened the windows of the Church to the fresh air of the modern world. This Twenty-First Ecumenical Council was the first to reflect a truly world Church. For three years Cardinals and Bishops from every continent and from nearly every nation on the globe assembled to discuss the nature of the Church and its mission to and in the world.

The Council leaders were acutely sensitive to the problems of a world polarized by ideologies and threatened by nuclear warfare. They witnessed first hand the effects of a spiraling arms race, environmental destruction, and the growing disparity between rich and poor. They also recognized that the Church, by virtue of the mission which Christ had entrusted to it, has a unique responsibility for shaping values and institutions in that world.

In many respects, Vatican II represented the end of one era and the beginning of a new era. The enthusiasm and energies of the Age of Enlightenment had been spent. This philosophical movement of the eighteenth century, marked by a rejection of traditional social, religious, and political ideas and an emphasis on rationalism, had culminated in the Holocaust in Europe and in a world sharply divided. These events had dashed hopes that secular society, based on human reason severed from religious faith, would lead to unending progress. Instead a misguided rationalism had unleashed forces which threatened to destroy the world.

The Church had turned inward in reaction to a rationalistic age which demeaned religious belief. Religion, more and more defined as a "private" affair between the individual and God, was relegated to a marginal role in secular society. At the same time, the Church channeled its energies outwardly to evangelize the "mission lands" of Africa, Asia, and Latin America.

During Vatican II, the Council leaders rejected that marginal role in society as inconsistent with the unique religious mission which Christ had given to his Church. They disclaimed for the Church any unique and proper mission in the political, economic, or social order. But in *The Church in the Modern World (Gaudium et Spes, 1965),* they affirmed that the specifically religious mission of the Church did give it "a function, a light, and an energy which can serve to structure and consolidate the human community according to the divine law. As a matter of fact, when circumstances of time and place create the need, it can and indeed should initiate activities on behalf of all people" (#42).

Yet the Council, in relating the Church to the wider society, did caution against any disrespect shown toward other views which were religiously founded. This was the message of the great statement *On Religious Freedom (Dignitatis Humanae, 1965),* a statement strongly influenced by the experience of the Church in the United States.

THE CHURCH AFTER THE SECOND VATICAN COUNCIL

The Faith That Does Justice

Since Vatican II, statements by Pope Paul VI and Pope John Paul II, by Synods of Bishops, and by regional and national conferences of Bishops have helped to clarify the role of the Church in meeting its new responsibilities in a rapidly changing world. The Popes and the Bishops have been acutely aware that the search for God's word in the events of history is not a simple task. They also have recognized that the Church has neither immediate nor universally valid solutions to all the complex and pressing problems of society.

Three documents in particular have contributed to the Church's present understanding of its new responsibilities. Pope Paul VI's encyclical letter *The Development of Peoples (Populorum Progressio, 1967)* responded to the cries of the world's poor and hungry and addressed the structural dimensions of global injustice. Speaking of the right of all to integral human development, he appealed to both rich and poor nations to work together in a spirit of solidarity to establish an order of justice and bring about the renewal of the temporal order. To encourage this noble enterprise he set up a Pontifical Commission on Justice and Peace.

The second document was the apostolic letter *A Call to Action (Octogesima Adveniens*, 1971*)*, which Paul VI wrote on the occasion of the eightieth anniversary of *On the Condition of Labor.* Here Paul VI acknowledged the difficulties inherent in establishing a just social order and pointed to the role of local Christian communities in meeting this responsibility.

It is up to the Christian communities to analyze with objectivity the situation which is proper to their own country, to shed on it the light of the Gospel's unalterable words and to draw principles of reflection, norms of judgment and directives for action from the social teaching of the Church (#4).

In effect Paul VI insisted that God calls Christians and communities to be both *hearers* and *doers* of the word. Christians who are faithful to the Gospel will be engaged in an ongoing "incarnational" process which involves three separate moments:

1. Evaluation and analysis of their contemporary situation.
2. Prayer, discernment, and reflection, bringing the light of the Gospel and the teachings of the Church to bear on the situation.
3. Pastoral action which fights injustices and works for the transformation of society, thus laboring to make the "reign" of God a reality.

Also in 1971, representatives of the world's Bishops gathered in a Synod in Rome and prepared the statement *Justice in the World.* In this third document, which illustrates the influence of a truly world Church, the Bishops identified the dynamism of the Gospel with the hopes of people for a better world. In what has become a well-known and frequently cited statement, they asserted:

Action on behalf of justice and participation in the transformation of the world fully appear to us as a constitutive dimension of the preaching of the Gospel, or in other words, of the Church's mission for the redemption of the human race and its liberation from every oppressive situation (#6).

This vision of the social mission of the Church, of a Church that "does" justice as an integral element of its faith, is slowly leavening the universal Church. It is manifest in the activities and teachings of regional and national conferences of Bishops, such as those of the U.S. Church and of the Latin American Church in Medellín (1968) and Puebla (1979). It is being proclaimed in the faith and actions of countless individuals, communities, and local churches throughout the world. Central to this vision, the Synod noted, is that the Church which would proclaim justice to the world must itself be seen to be just.

Evangelization and Justice

Pope Paul VI advanced the social teaching of the Church further in his *Evangelization in the Modern World (Evangelii Nuntiandi,* 1975). Here he emphasized that preaching the Gospel would be incomplete if it did not take into account human rights and the themes of family life, life in society, peace, justice, and development. Liberation—in both its spiritual and its temporal senses—must be proclaimed. The plan of the Redemption includes combating injustice.

This strong link between the Gospel and social justice has been emphasized repeatedly by Pope John Paul II. In his first encyclical letter, *Redeemer of Humankind (Redemptor Hominis,* 1979), he stated that when we put the human at the center then we see contemporary society in need of redemption. John Paul II challenged disrespect of the environment and an uncritical stance toward technological advance. *Rich in Mercy (Dives Misericordiae,* 1980) presented mercy as social love, demonstrating its close link to justice.

John Paul II's next important social teaching came in *On Human Work (Laborem Exercens,* 1981). "The priority of labor over capital" was enunciated as central to the just society. The Pope criticized an "economism" which would reduce humans to mere instruments of production. He called the workers' struggle for justice the dynamic element in contemporary society, emphasizing the need for greater "solidarity" around the world. *On Human Work* also takes up again a common theme in the Church's social teaching, the critique of liberal capitalism and the warning against collectivist socialism.

The Missionary Activity of the Church (Redemptoris Missio, 1990), John Paul II's encyclical that emphasizes the church's mission to non-Christians, confirms these teachings. The Pope highlights the necessity of proclaiming Christ as a means of restoring human dignity. He states the importance of individuals and the Church "taking courageous and prophetic stands in the face of the corruption of political or economic power" in order to "serve the poorest of the poor" (#43). *The Missionary Activity of the Church* also treats inculturation, liberation, ecumenical activity, human rights, and the value of witnessing to the Gospel. *One Hundred Years (Centesimus Annus,* 1991), John Paul II's most recent encyclical, teaches that the spread of Catholic social teaching itself is an "essential" part of the Church's missionary activity.

Application of this emphasis on the linkage between evangelization and justice has been effectively made by the Latin American bishops. In Medellín (1968) they presented Jesus as liberator from sin in both personal and social dimensions, and showed the consequences for the Church of a mission which promotes peace and justice. The Puebla document (1979) developed further the mission of evangelization and stressed the role of base communities and the laity. Evangelization and liberation were seen as integral.

Other examples of a Third World connection between the Christian vision and the reality of today's challenges are found in the 1981 statement of the Bishops of the African continent and the 1974 statement of the Bishops of Asia. The African statement presented a pastoral program for the local churches which included a strong emphasis on education for justice. At the national level, the need to speak out for justice was stressed; at the international level, an appeal was made for more just structures. In the Asian statement, the Bishops emphasized that evangelization requires a dialogue with the poor and that this dialogue must include a focus on the situations of injustice and oppression.

Further development in the social teaching of the Church can be found in two statements by Cardinal Joseph Ratzinger of the Congregation for the Defense of the Faith. *Instruction on Certain Aspects of the Theology of Liberation* (1984) and *Instruction on Christian Freedom and Liberation* (1986), both were released with the explicit approval of their contents by John Paul II. These statements can be seen as cautions against some strains of liberation theology—not, it should be noted in honesty, the main streams. But even more important, the Ratzinger documents reiterated the more recent emphasis of Catholic social teaching on the need for structural transformation in order to achieve social justice, on the centrality of the liberation theme itself in the biblical message and hence the entire Christian message, and on the preferential option for the poor.

John Paul II's *The Missionary Activity of the Church* affirms the importance of liberation to the Church's mission. The Pope acknowledges that liberation involves activity to alter situations of economic and political oppression. The encyclical notes the value of work for economic development and the promotion of human rights. The Pope cautions, however, that true liberation involves the *totality* of the human person and communities. He pleads for the complete and integral liberation of all humankind.

Peace, Justice, and Politics

The United States Catholic Church has taken seriously Paul VI's call to apply the social teachings to "the situation which is proper to their own country." A series of statements have come from the U.S. Conference of Catholic Bishops (USCCB), formerly known as the National Conference of Catholic Bishops (NCCB), and its policy arm, the United States Catholic Conference (USCC). The four most important statements form a "quartet" of pastoral letters, on the topics of racism (1979), peace (1983), economic justice (1986), and mission (1986). Basic to each pastoral letter is its foundation in the tradition of the social teaching enunciated by the Popes and Vatican II.

The U.S. Bishops address racism in *Brothers and Sisters to Us* (1979). This pastoral letter terms racism an "evil" that violates human dignity. Racism is manifested in contemporary life, the letter suggests, in a sense of indifference to the marginalized and an overemphasis on individualism. The Bishops call the U.S. Church and society to conversion and renewal. The letter advocates domestic and international policies that alleviate the tragic effects of racism.

The arms race and international tensions were addressed in *The Challenge of Peace: God's Promise and Our Response* (1983). The pastoral letter came twenty years after John XXIII's *Peace on Earth* and reiterated strongly the need to build the structures of peace. It stirred considerable controversy by reason of its challenge to the Reagan administration's defense policy, including its moral analysis of the stance of nuclear deterrence. While relying primarily on the tradition of the just war theory, the letter also emphasized the importance of the non-violent (pacifist) tradition. One consequence of the letter was that moral considerations have entered more widely into the politics of public debate over military defense policies.

The social justice aspects of topics such as unemployment, poverty, agriculture, and global interdependence were treated in *Economic Justice for All: Catholic Social Teaching and the U.S. Economy* (1986). As they moved into making specific policy recommendations, the U.S. Bishops repeated a significant distinction they had made earlier in the Peace Pastoral by acknowledging that their judgments and recommendations "do not carry the same moral authority as our statements of universal moral principles and formal church teaching" (#135). Their prudential judgments on specific economic issues have direct political consequences: they will, and are designed to, stimulate debate and dialogue. Central to the Economics Pastoral, rooted in its scriptural foundation, was the emphasis on the option for the poor.

The option for the poor came up again in *To the Ends of the Earth* (1986), when the U.S. Bishops spoke of a holistic approach to mission, one which necessarily includes liberation. A new self-understanding of the Church was stressed in this pastoral letter, with Church being essentially identified with mission in the widest sense. It is a significant commentary on the "seamless garment" character of Catholic social teaching that the Mission Pastoral said that the concern for mission springs from the sense of discipleship which has been articulated in the pastoral letters on peace and on economic justice.

Pope John Paul II, in *The Social Concerns of the Church (Sollicitudo Rei Socialis*, 1988), pushed the link between peace and justice further by emphasizing the plight of Third World development in terms of the harmful influence of superpower confrontation. Commemorating *The Development of Peoples,* John Paul II asserted that little or no development actually had occurred since Paul VI's strong call in 1968. He strongly criticized the desire for profit and the thirst for power, calling them "structures of sin." The Pope offered a solution in the direction of a politics of solidarity.

The most recent papal social encyclical, *One Hundred Years (Centesimus Annus,* 1991), advances Catholic social teaching even further. It articulates a "right to progress" which states that all people have the right to acquire and develop the skill and technology which will enable them to participate in the contemporary economy. The Pope states that the stronger nations have a duty to allow the weaker nations to assume their rightful place in the world. The encyclical, more so than any other document in Catholic social teaching, links its prescriptions for reform to the love that springs from belief in Gospel values. The Pope understands the primary role of the Church as one of forming human minds and hearts according to these Gospel values.

3

A SHIFTING SOCIAL APPROACH

The body of Catholic social teaching is by no means a fixed set of tightly developed doctrine. Rather, it is a collection of key themes which has evolved in response to the challenges of the day. Rooted in biblical orientations and reflections on Christian tradition, the social teaching shows a lively evolution marked by shifts both in *attitude* and *methodology*. What informs the teaching of John Paul II today differs from what informed the teaching of Leo XIII almost a century ago—even though both ground their message in the same faith in the God revealed by and in Jesus Christ. This means that the approach taken in the Church's social teaching has been undergoing some significant shifting that we should pay attention to in order to appreciate its contemporary relevance.

SHIFTS IN ATTITUDE

The Second Vatican Council marked a new period in the life of the Church. One fundamental aspect of this new period was a change in the Church's attitude toward the world. Such a change has had profound consequences for the themes and emphases of the Church's social teaching. Philip Land, S.J., of the Center of Concern, has identified four distinct aspects in this change in attitude (see "Catholic Social Teaching: 1891–1981," *Center Focus*, no. 43, May 1981). Although Land's article is more than two decades old, Catholic social teaching has continued to evolve in the directions he indicated.

1. **An assault on political apathy.** Many Church leaders, theologians, and loyal critics continue to ask how it was possible for the Church to be largely silent and passive in the face of the atrocities of the Second World War. The answer at least in part is that the Church and religion had become confined to the private arena. Rejecting this privatization and the political apathy it

engenders, Vatican II recognized that the Church shares responsibility for secular as well as for religious history. Pope Paul VI insisted in *A Call to Action* that politics is a "vocation" aimed at the transformation of society. John Paul II stressed in *The Missionary Activity of the Church* that individual Christians, Christian communities, and the Church itself must be prepared to take "prophetic stands" in situations of political or economic corruption.

2. **A commitment to the "humanization" of life.** The Council emphasized the Church's responsibility for the world, a world which God created and Jesus walked upon. Moreover, as the Council leaders affirmed and as Pope John Paul II stated in *On Human Work,* people can rightly consider that they are continuing the Creator's work through their own labor and contributing to the realization in history of the divine plan. From these attitudes a respect develops for the rightful autonomy of the secular world.

3. **A commitment to world justice.** The Bishops in their 1971 Synod statement, *Justice in the World,* urged that justice be sought at all levels of society but especially between rich and powerful nations and those that are poor and weak. The Bishops declared that the doing of justice is a "constitutive dimension of the preaching of the Gospel" (#6). A truly global vision is the hallmark of the Christian. This vision is given voice in *One Hundred Years* in which Pope John Paul II grapples with issues, concerns, and situations challenging the First, Second, and Third Worlds.

4. **Preferential option for the poor.** The Church has always understood that Christ identifies with the poor and underprivileged. But it now looks at this truth with new urgency and new pastoral consequences. In reading the "signs of the times," Christians see God's face above all in the faces of suffering and wounded people. Consequently, fidelity to Christ requires an identification with and an "option" for the poor. In the last few years this conviction has become a priority for the Church in its theological reflection and pastoral action. Originally an insight of the Latin American Church, the option for the poor has been assumed by the universal Church in the statements of John Paul II. It has had a strong influence on the U.S. Bishops' Economics Pastoral.

SHIFTS IN METHODOLOGY

Several methodological changes have accompanied the attitudinal changes noted above. Land identifies five significant shifts in the methodology of the Church's social teaching.

1. **Imaging the Church as the "People of God."** Vatican II, in *The Nature of the Church (Lumen Gentium, 1964),* emphasized the Church as "People

of God." This biblical image holds important implications not only for ecclesiology, but also for the Church's approach to the social order. The Church as "People of God" lifts the faithful from a passive role to an active role in defining and shaping their history in the contemporary world. But the Church does not claim any special, unique competence in technical questions. It views its own social teaching as more of an orientation and a motivating force than as a model for solving social problems. The Church does not possess all the answers, but searches for them in cooperation with others. As Paul VI indicated in *A Call to Action* (#4), and John Paul affirmed in *The Missionary Activity of the Church,* it is up to local Christian communities to join others of good will in seeking solutions to pressing social questions.

2. **Reading the "signs of the times."** It is a basic Christian belief that God continues to speak in and through human history. This truth was reaffirmed by Vatican II. Consequently, the Church has "the duty of scrutinizing the signs of the times and of interpreting them in the light of the gospel" *(The Church in the Modern World, #4).* This statement in effect introduced a new method of "doing" theology.

The Church looks to the world and discovers there God's presence. Signs both reveal God's presence in the world and manifest God's designs for the world. Implicit in this truth is that theology must go beyond the purely deductive and speculative. History ceases to be the mere context for the application of binding principles, which are derived uniquely from speculative and philosophical reasoning. It becomes the place of ongoing revelation.

3. **The movement away from a narrow adherence to natural law to a greater reliance on Scripture.** As the social teaching has shifted from the deductive to the inductive and the historical, there has been a movement away from a rigidly interpreted natural law ethic. The defined absolutes of an earlier natural law have been replaced by the search for the objectively true, which is seen to be the objectively human insofar as that can be disclosed.

This search for the objectively human is rooted in experience and embraces an holistic approach to human decision making. External truths, insofar as these can be possessed, need to be filtered through personal experiences, observation, memory, and general societal history. This process of human decision making necessarily involves the struggle to understand the full human reality and to discover the call of God in the midst of that reality.

Scripture has become the new touchstone for Catholic social teaching. Pope John Paul II has used Scripture in his encyclicals more extensively than any of his predecessors. In *On Human Work,* he bases his understanding of the dignity of the human person and human work on insights contained in Genesis. In *One Hundred Years,* he rests his assertion of shared responsibility for all humanity on principles contained in the Gospels of Matthew and Luke.

4. **The primacy of love.** Reason was the primary shaper of the Church's earlier formulation of social teaching. In recent decades, however, the social teaching has been increasingly shaped by the primacy of love. The primacy of love has three meanings in this context. First, love is at the heart of the virtue of justice and brings the actions of justice to their fullest potential, meaning, and life. Second, love is the motivation to act on behalf of justice. Third, the fundamental option of love, which the heart makes for God as the ground of our being, produces moral action. Reason is not discarded in the social teachings, but put in its proper place.

5. **An orientation to pastoral planning and action.** The evolving methodology of the Church's social teaching is also praxis-oriented. Praxis, the action that comes out of reflection and leads back to reflection, can be viewed as the end result of an option which one makes in the struggle for justice. The corollary is that correct action ("orthopraxis") completes correct doctrine ("orthodoxy").

The earlier methodology of Catholic social teaching often led to social idealism. It isolated reason from a relationship of dialogue with experience, commitment, and action. But from the praxis side, the starting point of pastoral and social reflection is people in their struggle, in their needs, and in their hopes. Praxis thus becomes a true force for understanding and developing all authentic social teaching.

4

MAJOR LESSONS OF CATHOLIC SOCIAL TEACHING

Theological Context: Reading the Signs of the Times. A foundational conviction underlying Catholic social teaching is that God is at work in human history. This was true in biblical times; it is true today. It is true in places the Gospel has been embraced; and it is true in places and among people who have never heard of the Gospel or of Jesus the Christ. God is at work healing and redeeming human history and inviting all people to participate in that work. Perceiving the historical action of God and discerning God's invitation are often now referred to as "reading the signs of the times."

The term "signs of the times" in contemporary Catholic social thought is a term based upon Jesus' statement to the Pharisees and Sadducees in Matthew 16:4—"You know how to read the face of the sky, but you cannot read the signs of the times." Pope John XXIII made the first use of the term in modern Catholic social teaching to refer to the principal characteristics of the age that are emerging from the collective consciousness of the human community in the form of shared understandings and social movements. In *Peace on Earth (Pacem in Terris),* John XXIII identified the women's movement, the movement for workers' rights, and the ending of colonialism as important "signs of the times."

The Second Vatican Council embraced the notion, bringing it to the heart of the Church's mission.

> The Church seeks but a solitary goal: to carry forward the work of Christ Himself under the lead of the befriending Spirit. And Christ entered this world to give witness to the truth, to rescue and not to sit in judgment, to serve and not to be served. To carry out such a task, the Church has always had the duty of scrutinizing the signs of the times

and of interpreting them in the light of the Gospel. *(The Church in the Modern World [Gaudium et Spes])*

The "signs of the times," then, embody and reflect the movement of the Holy Spirit in human history working to bring about the redemption of peoples and the fuller realization of the Reign of God. Interpreting the "signs of the times" requires prayerful discernment within the Christian community and in dialogue with all people of good will. The criteria for this discernment involve the coherence of the contemporary "signs of the times" with the Gospels, the Christian understanding of human nature, and the common good.

Catholic Social Teaching. The growing body of official Catholic social teaching, beginning with *On the Condition of Labor (Rerum Novarum)*, comprises a collection of efforts by the Church to read the "signs of the times" in industrial life. During this period, certain values and principles have emerged as consistent recurrent themes offering special insight into what the faith community believes God is doing and inviting us to do in this historical period.

There have been various attempts through the years to summarize these key themes of Catholic social teaching. The first editions of this book identified ten major lessons; later editions went to twelve, and then to fourteen. The Center of Concern's website now identifies more than twenty. In 1999 the U.S. Conference of Catholic Bishops (USCCB) reversed the trend and distilled seven general principles.

A smaller number of principles is easier to learn and remember. Its disadvantage, however, is that the principles must be stated in very general, abstract terms. It seems valuable, therefore, to build upon the foundation of the seven core principles popularized by USCCB while expanding upon each to identify important related principles and to illustrate more clearly their important implications for life in today's world.

Within this context, the following principles are at the foundation of Catholic social thought in its efforts to read the "signs of these times."

1. The Dignity of the Human Person

Major Areas of Concern
—Authentic Human Development
—Love of God, Love of Neighbor
—Love and Justice
—Dialogue

THE DIGNITY OF THE HUMAN PERSON. *As children of God created in God's image, human persons have a preeminent place in creation. Human dignity is the result of human existence. It is not earned by achievements or bestowed by any authorities other than God. It is not dependent on race, creed, color, economic class, political power, social status, culture, personal abilities, gender, sexual orientation or any other dimensions by which people discriminate social groupings. There is a unique and sacred worth that is present in each person simply because she or he exists. The germinal aptitudes and abilities each person possesses at birth constitute a divine vocation, a specific and unique calling to further the development of human society as a whole. (The Development of Peoples [Populorum Progressio])*

Authentic Human Development. For Catholic social thought, the sacred character of human dignity clearly demands that authentic human development not be understood simply as economic development. Full and authentic human development embraces the social, cultural, political and spiritual dimensions of human life as well. It involves developing one's skills and gifts for service to the common good.

Because of this, no form of government should be dominated by the concerns and established laws of economic development alone. The situation that exists today at the level of global governance, for example, in which the World Trade Organization is the most powerful institution and trade policy dominates global policy making, is a violation of authentic human development and an affront to human dignity that must be corrected.

More recent Catholic social teaching has even stressed that economic development can impede authentic human development. Pope Paul VI pointed out that greed is the most blatant form of moral underdevelopment *(The Development of Peoples [Populorum Progressio])*. Pope John Paul II has argued that the drive to "have" possessions can be the worst enemy to growth in the depth and quality of personal "being." He cites as one of the great challenges to authentic human development the reality of the miseries of poverty or economic underdevelopment existing side-by-side with the inadmissible superdevelopment which involves consumerism and waste. *(The Social Concerns of the Church [Sollicitudo Rei Socialis])*.

True human development involves a commitment of solidarity with all people, especially with those in poverty and situations of oppression. It is a mistake, then, from the perspective of Catholic social thought, to call wealthy nations that do not live and work in effective solidarity with those in poverty "developed nations."

Love of God, Love of Neighbor. Love of God and love of neighbor have been closely linked throughout the Judeo-Christian traditions. They have been conceived in a variety of different relationships over time.

For some people, love of neighbor is the command given us by God. If we love God, we will be obedient and love our neighbor. For some, it is important to focus on love of God; in the relationship developed, God will lead us to love for our neighbor. For some, for example the apostle John, if we do not love our neighbor, our claim to love God is a lie. For some, very practical caring for the neighbor is an embodiment of effective love of God. For some, love of God and neighbor are one and the same because God is in the neighbor and the neighbor is in God.

Catholic social thought is itself a witness to the Church's belief that the two cannot be separated. Both are indispensable to authentic human development. Love of neighbor shown in work for social justice is essential to love of God; and love of God and neighbor are essential to the work for justice. Human dignity is grounded in God's creative love and invites our love.

Love and Justice. It is not uncommon, in ordinary conversation, to hear love and justice or charity and justice contrasted. In this view, love and charity are personal, generous, free, life-giving, Christian. They are distinguished sharply from justice which is seen as impersonal, harsh, punitive, socially desirable, but secular. This is not the position of authentic Catholic Christian teaching.

In Catholic social thought, love of neighbor is an absolute demand for justice, because charity must manifest itself in actions and structures which respect human dignity, protect human rights and facilitate human development. To promote justice is to transform structures which block love *(Justice in the World)*. To love each and every person, as Jesus commands us to do, requires that we establish structures of justice which support and liberate all peoples. As the 1971 Synod of Bishops testified in *Justice in the World*: "Action on behalf of justice and participation in the transformation of the world fully appear to us as a constitutive dimension of the preaching of the Gospel, or in other words, of the Church's mission for the redemption of the human race and its liberation from every oppressive situation."

Dialogue. The sacred dignity of each person and the call to love one's neighbor as an essential element of one's love of God combine to demand that all differences be explored and all conflicts be addressed through respectful dialogue. This applies to religious differences as well as political, economic, social and cultural ones. Only through patient, respectful dialogue do people grow beyond the limitations of their experience, perceptions, opinions and values. Each person is a unique part of the tapestry of creation, of the mosaic of the human family. Only through dialogue can new levels of understanding and appreciation be achieved in the human community. The conditions for dialogue are destroyed and human dignity violated when demonizing rhetoric is used in times of conflict.

2. The Dignity of Work

Major Areas of Concern
—The Priority of Labor over Capital
—Religious and Social Development

THE DIGNITY OF WORK. *While work is not the source of human dignity, it is the means by which persons express and develop both being and dignity. Persons are the subjects of work and are not to be looked upon simply as a means of production or a human form of capital. Work must be organized to serve the workers' humanity, support their family life, and increase the common good of the human community—the three purposes of work. Workers have the right to organize and form unions to achieve these goals. (On Human Work [Laborem Exercens])*

The Priority of Labor over Capital. Products and technologies are the fruits of work and part of the universal heritage of the human family. People always take priority over products, profits, and production systems *(On Human Work [Laborem Exercens])*. The primary concern must always be with the development and well-being of the workers, not the efficiency, productivity, profits and competitiveness of the business, though these are important to its survival. Any business that does not enhance its workers and serve the common good is a moral failure no matter how healthy its financial bottom line appears. This is a central issue of justice in the processes of globalization of production and trade.

The fundamental question to ask about economic development, then, is "What is it doing to people? What is it doing for people? What is it enabling people to do themselves and to participate in?" *(Economic Justice for All)*.

Religious and Social Development. The results or objects of work, the human construction of the world, is not "secular" in the sense of being outside of God's plan or activity. As the process of development of human persons and communities, it is intimately involved with the dynamic of the Reign of God. Human products and services express personal and community values and play a part in the future of the people's lives, forming the context and the structures that shape subsequent human development. Therefore, the sacred and the secular are not distinct realms; faith and justice are necessarily linked together. And they pertain to every part of life *(The Church in the Modern World [Gaudium et Spes], One Hundred Years [Centesimus Annus])*.

3. The Person in Community

Major Areas of Concern
—Common Good
—Human Freedom/Social Structures
—Structures of Sin/Structures of
   Grace
—Liberation
—Participation
—The Role of the Church

THE PERSON IN COMMUNITY. *Human dignity can be recognized, developed and protected only in community with others. Each person is brother or sister to every other and can develop as a healthy human person only in a community of relationships rooted in love and justice. The foundational community for each person is his or her immediate family; the full community of each is the extended family of the whole human race through history within the larger community of created being. Each person benefits from the efforts of earlier generations and of their contemporaries and are therefore under obligation to them as well. (The Development of Peoples [Populorum Progressio])*

Common Good. The common good is the total of all those conditions of social living—economic, political, sociological and cultural—which make it possible for women and men readily and fully to achieve the perfection of their humanity. Individual rights are always experienced within the context of the promotion of the common good.

In Catholic social thought, the common good is not simply the sum of individual goods. It is not, as in utilitarian ethics, the sum of the good of the greatest number of people. That approach presumes that some people will, realistically, be left out or excluded from the benefits of social advance—and accepts that fact. Catholic social thought emphasizes and insists upon the participation of each and every person in the common good. It stands in challenging contrast to many contemporary cultures' heightened individualism.

Catholic social thought's vision of promoting the common good involves working on developing in society all those conditions of social living through which each and every person can be enabled to achieve their authentic human development more fully.

At the national level, promoting community and the common good requires creating employment for all, caring for the less privileged, and providing for the future. At the global level, it increasingly requires analogous interventions on behalf of the whole human family *(Centesimus Annus)*.

Human Freedom/Social Structures. Each person is born into a social context of technologies, community values, shared interpretations of life, organizations of services and opportunities for development. This complex context or set of social and cultural structures is essential to community living and individual development. Personal freedom emerges and is shaped within it.

At times that process is easy and supportive; at others it is conflictual. This continual interplay can serve to keep social structures flexible and responsive to human needs and development; it can also suppress and even destroy legitimate human aspirations and growth. Any set of social and cultural structures should, in fact, be presumed to be doing both.

Structures of Sin/Structures of Grace. Looked at from a faith-based moral perspective, structures that support and facilitate authentic human development can be called structures of grace. Those that obstruct authentic development and obscure the universal common good are structures of sin. While both types begin in individual acts, they are gradually consolidated into structures that make change more difficult. They then influence and shape the graced or sinful acts of others.

Pope John Paul II identifies two major and intertwined structures of sin in contemporary life: "on the one hand, the all-consuming desire for profit, and on the other, the thirst for power with the intention of imposing one's will upon others" *(The Social Concerns of the Church [Sollicitudo Rei Socialis])*.

Liberation. Liberation from oppressive social, political and economic situations and structures is an important part of the Church's activity. Liberation, however, must encompass the entire person, including the spiritual and religious dimensions.

Liberation theology began in Latin America in response to the slavery of poverty that still afflicts the vast majority of people there. It highlighted the uneven and unjust power relationships that have created the poverty, thereby identifying much poverty as the result of oppression rather than as evidence of a simple lack of development, so-called "underdevelopment." Liberation theology has spread around the world, stimulating theological reflection on the forms of oppression and slavery to be found in different cultures and social contexts.

In the 1980s, some Vatican offices voiced concerns because liberation theology did not address the issues of atheism and nihilism that plagued Europe and did not adequately distance itself from the atheistic foundations of the Marxist analysis that it embraced.

Vatican concerns, at this point, have been assuaged, and the major liberation theologians continue their important service of the Church's struggle
for global liberation and justice. Perhaps the most important contributions
of this theological stream or school have been its starting point in the experience of the oppressed and those in poverty, as well as its methodology of
biblically based reflection on that experience to discern God's call in our
midst. Liberation motifs play an important part in Catholic social thought
today.

Participation. The opportunity for democratic participation in decision
making is the best way to respect the dignity and liberty of people. Government is one of the major instruments by which people cooperate in order to
achieve the common good. Fostering the international common good
requires frameworks and opportunities for participation in international
organizations as well.

Here Catholic social teaching offers guidance for the political struggles
shaping the institutions and structures of international life at the beginning
of the twenty-first century. At the global level, smaller and poorer nations
do not yet have the ability to make their needs and concerns effectively
heard in the financial and trade decisions that affect their well-being. Civil
society organizations that are essential to holding national and international institutions accountable are given very little opportunity to participate in the financial and trade policy decision processes.

At the national level, it is too often those with the greatest wealth and
power that dominate the selection of political candidates and the communication of campaign messages. Efforts for campaign finance reform are
intended to restore the ability of ordinary citizens to participate in the decisions that will shape their lives.

Role of the Church. The Church is called to be a sacrament of God's
Reign, a visible embodiment of the type of community God is working to
bring about. In accordance with that ideal, the human rights of all within
the Church must be respected, with special attention to the rights of women
and lay people *(Justice in the World)*.

This sacred mission challenges the Church at each moment to be a discerning community grappling with the problems of the larger human community, witnessing to justice, working to heal, redeem and transform the
institutions, policies and patterns by which the people of the planet live
with each other and with the whole earth community.

The actual history of the Church is, unfortunately, characterized by many
scandals and human rights abuses. Some argue these are simply the result of
the sins of individuals within the Church; others argue that the structures of
the Church reflect the limitations and sinfulness of the cultures in which it
has developed. Either way, Catholic social teaching acknowledges that the

Church's credibility and moral authority in matters of justice are under-mined when it is not itself just *(Justice in the World)*.

4. Rights and Responsibilities

Major Areas of Concern
—Human Rights
—Responsibilities
—Private Property/Social Mortgage
—Resisting Market Idolatry
—The Role of Government
—The Principle of Subsidiarity

RIGHTS AND RESPONSIBILITIES. Human rights flow from the intrinsic sacred dignity of the person in his or her vocation to serve the community. They are to be recognized by communities and governments; they do not derive from the dictates of governments. Nor are they earned or won by successful competition in the marketplace. It is the responsibility of each to respect and protect the human rights of all.

Human Rights. The Catholic social tradition presents its most extensive delineation of human rights in Pope John XXIII's encyclical *Peace on Earth (Pacem in Terris)*. They include basic economic, social and cultural rights such as the rights to life, food, clothing, shelter, health care, education, work or employment with a just and sufficient wage, and leisure—all the basic human needs. And they include also the civil and political rights to the social goods of freedom of speech, religion, association, migration, and participation in society.

Economic, social and cultural rights require special attention in this his-torical period in which globalization threatens cultural domination by the more powerful, media-rich nations of the West and is increasing the gap between the minority who are wealthy and the vast majority who are trapped in debilitating poverty.

The United Nations Covenant of Economic, Social and Cultural Rights has not been ratified by the United States and these rights are not recognized in U.S. law and culture. The U.S. Bishops have called for "A New American Experiment" to enshrine these rights in the culture and legal systems of the United States and in its relationships with the rest of the human community *(Economic Justice for All)*.

Responsibilities. In Catholic social thought, the full panoply of human rights implies extensive responsibilities. The development of each person, the honoring of her or his rights, and the common good of all the human family are the responsibility of each and of all. Each person is the heir of previous generations and the beneficiary of contemporaries. This grounds the responsibility to contribute back to the well-being of contemporaries and that of generations to come *(Mother and Teacher [Mater et Magistra], Economic Justice for All)*. That fundamental responsibility is meant to guide each person's and each organization's participation in society.

Both Pope Leo XIII *(On the Condition of Labor)* and Pope Paul VI *(The Development of Peoples)* made clear that these responsibilities establish criteria for the justice of contracts and treaty agreements that go beyond simple participation or mutual consent. Contracts that do not respect the economic, social and cultural rights as well as the civil and political rights of all the participants and those affected by them are unjust. The development of global trade or governance systems must guarantee that the full human rights of all, especially those in poverty, are protected and that they have what they need to survive and develop and contribute back to the community. Especially when agreements are between unequal partners, it is necessary to evaluate their justice by these criteria very carefully.

Private Property/Social Mortgage. One of the first human rights and responsibilities to be discussed in modern Catholic social teaching is the right to private property. That right was under attack by Communism at the time that Pope Leo XIII wrote *On the Condition of Labor (Rerum Novarum)* in 1891. Its treatment in the evolving modern tradition of Catholic social teaching provides a good illustration of the way in which rights and responsibilities are always held in dynamic tension.

In Catholic social teaching, everyone has a right to private property. Property is important to human development and is, therefore, a right that should be defended and protected. This is an essential value of market societies. It has long been used to legitimate disparities in wealth within and among societies.

For Catholic social tradition, however, the right to private property is *not* an absolute right. It is limited by the common purpose of all goods: to serve the needs and development of the whole human community. Recent social teaching documents have retrieved the strong position held in the first centuries of the Church's life: no one has the right to accumulate more private property than he or she needs while others on the planet lack the very basics for survival and development. Everyone has a right to a share of earthly goods adequate for one's personal development and for that of his or her family. Pope John Paul II speaks of this as the social mortgage that exists on all private property *(Economic Justice for All, The Social Concerns of the Church [Sollicitudo Rei Socialis], One Hundred Years [Centesimus Annus])*.

This notion of a social mortgage has very important implications for issues of intellectual property rights and patents. Neither should be allowed to prevent people from getting the food and medicines they need to survive.

The genetic modification of seed crops and the severe impact of HIV/AIDS, tuberculosis and malaria have forced these issues to the forefront of international debate.

Resisting Market Idolatry. Pope John Paul II has also been most clear in insisting that, while markets can be effective and efficient instruments for developing and distributing resources, there are certain things that must not ultimately be subject to market dynamics. Since markets do not respond to people without adequate purchasing power, it is a "strict duty of justice and truth" to guarantee that anything essential to survival and to developing the ability to contribute back to the community must not be simply under market control *(One Hundred Years [Centesimus Annus])*.

In addition, there are common goods such as the natural and human environments that cannot and should not be the subject of market mechanisms. They are not mere commodities. They "cannot and must not be bought or sold" *(One Hundred Years [Centesimus Annus])*.

The Role of Government. Catholic social thought thus envisions a complex, layered society founded on individual initiative and shared responsibility, which expresses itself through participation in a vast variety of organizations. The interrelationships of those organizations must be coordinated and regulated in such a way that they actually serve the common good of all—locally, nationally, globally—and protect the common goods of the human community. That coordination and regulation constitute the role of government.

The Principle of Subsidiarity. The principle guiding all these complex social relationships and defining the proper activities of governments is the "principle of subsidiarity," first articulated by Pope Pius XI in 1931 *(The Reconstruction of the Social Order [Quadragesimo Anno])*. It is a two-edged instrument. It insists that it is wrong for higher levels of social organization or government to do for individuals and groups what they can accomplish by their own initiative and hard work. Social activity is meant to enable the participants to develop themselves and care for their families and communities. On this edge, the principle of subsidiarity supports "grassroots" or "bottom up" forms of social development.

On the other edge, subsidiarity also requires that what individuals and local organizations cannot do for themselves to secure the common good must be done by higher forms of social organization or government. The Catholic social vision, while promoting "bottom up" approaches to development, does not accept the sophism that the government which governs least governs best. It demands higher levels of organization and authority when lower ones cannot protect and support the development of each person and serve the common good of all.

This is true even at the global level. Church leaders since at least Pope John XXIII in the early 1960s have pointed out the historic need for global government to provide for the universal common good of the whole human family—arguing for it on the basis of the principle of subsidiarity *(Peace on Earth [Pacem in Terris], The Development of Peoples [Populorum Progressio], One Hundred Years [Centesimus Annus])*.

5. Option for Those in Poverty

> **Major Area of Concern**
> —*Biblical Justice*

OPTION FOR THOSE IN POVERTY. *From the Jubilee vision laid out in the Book of Leviticus through the passionate proclamations of the Hebrew prophets and Jesus' identification of his vocation as "bringing good news to the poor . . . and proclaiming the year of God's Jubilee" (Luke 4:16–19), people in poverty have been at the heart of the Judeo-Christian social vision. They are the people most often forgotten, exploited and marginalized in societies. Their sacred dignity and authentic development are most likely to be overlooked or abused. They are the people who experience and reveal the failings and shortcomings of our social systems. Their experiences, insights and concerns offer important evidence in the search for the more just systems of social life to which God is calling the human community.*

As early as 1931, Pope Pius XI warned of the serious danger of the consolidation of wealth which is the natural result of the unregulated free market system. The market does not reward attention to all needs in society. It responds only to the needs and desires of those with the resources to reward those who serve them. Those in poverty are excluded. The more the control of wealth is consolidated in the hands of a few, the more the majority of people are deprived of their basic needs and desires and are excluded from meaningful participation in society.

As the gap grows between the wealthy and those in poverty, social unrest is inevitable, leading far too often to the violent conflict of crime, terrorism, or war. Since the market is such a central and strong social institution, it is important for the sake of the common good to give special attention and concern to the needs of those in poverty, those whom the market excludes and ignores.

Another stream of Catholic social tradition calling for solidarity with those in poverty finds its origins in the warnings of the Gospel of Luke

about the dangers of wealth for those people who have it. Pope John Paul II
has created the term "inadmissible superdevelopment" to focus attention
upon the "excessive availability of every kind of material goods" for the
benefit of a small segment of society globally *(The Social Concerns of the
Church [Sollicitudo Rei Socialis])*. The danger he points to is not merely
that the amassing of wealth and consumer goods might be used to oppress
others. It is also that this condition breeds greed, exaggerated self importance and consumerism, the preoccupation with "having" rather than
"being," the addiction to things that desensitizes people to the conditions
and needs of their sisters and brothers around the planet, thereby under-
mining and preventing their own authentic human development.

Biblical Justice. Justice in the biblical sense sums up many of these same
values and principles. It is achieved when each person—especially those persons in poverty or on the margins of society—has what she or he needs to
survive, to develop and thrive, and to give back to the community. It recognizes the right of each person to share in the goods of creation to that
extent.

The more common contemporary understanding of justice as equality of
opportunity is not adequate to define true biblical justice. While valuing
and embracing equal opportunity as an important element, biblical justice
recognizes that certain fundamental needs for food, health, education, and
so on must be fulfilled for anyone to be able to respond to opportunities
made available. The claim to being a self-made individual who only requires
equal opportunities for a situation to be just is naively uninformed about
the nature of human life.

6. Solidarity

Major Areas of Concern
—*Unity of Humanity*
—*Peacemaking*
—*Pacifism or Non-Violence*
—*Just War*

SOLIDARITY. *We all belong to one human family. As such we have
mutual obligations to promote the rights and development of all people
across communities, nations and the world, irrespective of national
boundaries. In particular, the rich nations have responsibilities toward
the poor nations, and people with wealth and resources are linked in*

the divine economy with those who lack them. Those who remain untouched or unchanged by the suffering of their brothers and sisters around the world are suffering from serious spiritual underdevelopment. They need solidarity for their own salvation. The structures of the international order must reflect true biblical justice. And conflicts should always be resolved in the most peaceful ways available, ways which respect and build solidarity among peoples.

Unity of Humanity. From the very beginnings of the Catholic social tradition through its latest utterances, all of humanity—every man, woman and child—is understood to be one family under God. Human dignity is the foundation of all rights, privileges and responsibilities. Divisions of the one human community into we/they, while useful for developing identity and cultures, must not be allowed to become divisions for privilege or conflict.

The core truth of Catholic social thought is the recognition that we are all one in being children of God. No one's fulfilment and salvation can be completely isolated from any other in the web of existence. Each depends ultimately on solidarity in the fulfilment and salvation of all. Catholic social thought challenges us to promote that vision, which is essential to the Gospel of Christ, and to develop principles to guide the achievement of that reality in human society.

Peacemaking. Peace is the fruit of justice and is dependent upon solidarity and right order among humans and among nations. Catholic social thought demands an end to the arms race and widespread trafficking in arms. Progressive disarmament is essential to future security. In order to promote peace and the conditions of peace, an effective international authority is necessary *(Peace on Earth [Pacem in Terris]).*

Christian tradition bears witness to two approaches to peacemaking: pacifism or non-violence and just war theory. Both approaches share the presumption against using military force to settle disputes. But the just war theory does define some situations in which war is legitimate as a last resort and in self defense while the pacifist tradition insists that peace can only be achieved through peaceful means.

The U.S. Bishops argued that the two approaches support and complement one another, each preserving the other from distortion *(The Challenge of Peace).* Catholic social teaching generally holds now, in an age of destructive technological warfare, that analysis from the viewpoint of non-violence and analysis from the viewpoint of just war teaching often converge in declaring war illegitimate.

Pacifism or Non-Violence. The image of the warrior God so prominent in parts of the Hebrew scriptures disappears completely in the Christian scriptures. Jesus proclaimed the Reign of God's love and peace. He distanced himself from the Zealots who sought to foment armed revolution against the Roman occupiers.

In 1963, Pope John XXIII called for an end to the arms race *(Peace on Earth [Pacem in Terris])*. Two years later, the Second Vatican Council pointed to the need for a "completely fresh reappraisal of war" *(The Church in the Modern World [Gaudium et Spes])*.

The U.S. bishops, in their 1983 pastoral letter on war and peace, stressed the importance of "the support for the pacifist option for individuals in the teaching of Vatican II and the reaffirmation that the popes have given to non-violent witness since the time of the Council" *(The Challenge of Peace: God's Promise and Our Response)*. The bishops suggest that the new historical moment in which modern weapons have magnified the horrors of war has brought the tradition of Christian non-violence back into prominence, highlighting its interdependence with just war teaching.

Just War. Although there is a presumption against the use of force at the foundations of the just war tradition, there is also acceptance of the position that sometimes the use of force is required. As a result, the tradition has evolved guidelines to help determine when war might be justified and how it could be waged in a just manner.

The danger in contemporary public discourse is that the presumption against force is too often shunted aside in the social and political crises of the moment. At the first signs of conflict, discussion of the just war principles begins in the public arena. That actually violates the spirit (and letter) of the principles by devaluing the insistence on exploring every peaceful means before considering violent conflict.

In addition, those in government who have the responsibility for building public support for war efforts have learned to use—and in some cases to manipulate—just war concepts in order to claim legitimacy for their actions. There is need for more serious public discussion of the use of just war theory in propaganda efforts to build public support for war. The Church risks the integrity of its mission for peace by the way it involves itself in the public debate.

The just war tradition's criteria for entering into war *(Jus ad Bellum)* are:

1. just cause,
2. competent authority,
3. comparative justice,
4. right intention,
5. last resort,
6. probability of success,
7. proportionality.

The just war tradition's criteria governing how to wage war *(Jus in Bello)*, once the decision has been made to enter into it, are:

1. Proportionality in level of aggression,
2. Immunity for non-combatants and non-military targets *(The Challenge of Peace)*.

In attempting to determine the legitimacy of a specific war with Just War criteria, Catholic social tradition considers it of the utmost importance to consider the poor and the helpless, for they are usually the ones who have the least to gain and the most to lose when war's violence touches their lives *(The Challenge of Peace)*. It calls for assessing the costs of weapons systems, the arms race, the impact on social spending for those most in need, the social climate of insecurity created, the danger of error and miscalculation, the danger of retaliation, and so on *(The Challenge of Peace)*.

Pope John Paul II pleaded with humanity in his "World Day of Peace Message" in 1982: "In view of the difference between classical warfare and nuclear or bacteriological war—a difference so to speak of nature—and in view of the scandal of the arms race seen against the background of the needs of the Third World, this right [of defense], which is very real in principle, only underlines the urgency of the world society to equip itself with effective means of negotiation. In this way the nuclear terror that haunts our time can encourage us to enrich our common heritage with a very simple discovery that is within our reach, namely, that war is the most barbarous and least effective way of resolving conflicts."

7. Care for Creation

CARE FOR CREATION. *People are to respect and share the resources of the earth, since we are all part of the community of creation. By our work we are co-creators in the continuing development of the earth. Catholic social thought has explicitly addressed environmental and ecological concerns only in rather recent times. But the concern for respecting, sharing and caring for creation has always been part of the tradition. Recent statements on the importance of environmentally and socially sustainable patterns of consumption and development have built solidly upon that part of the tradition.*

This vision is rooted solidly in the Judeo-Christian scriptures. Still, Catholic social thought has explicitly addressed environmental and ecological concerns only in rather recent times. As it became clear that exploitation and disruption of intricate natural systems could and did have serious consequences across all boundaries, the Second Vatican Council, episcopal synods, encyclicals, and other Vatican publications began to address them. They note the need for a unified moral vision, a global ethic, and global solidarity in addressing ecological problems.

The statements address a number of specific ecological concerns, most notably food production, water, and chemical hazards. While there is adequate food produced to feed the human community, more than 840 million people face various stages of starvation. They have a right to food security, the ability to produce their own food or to buy it. The human community must also increase its efforts to protect food-producing regions from desertification and erosion.

Water is essential to human life and dignity. Without an adequate water supply, there can be no real development. Many expect water to be the next issue over which great international conflicts arise. The peoples of the earth must cooperate in ending the human activities that pollute land and water and affect rain patterns.

Chemical pollution is also a serious danger to global development. Rich nations have a serious moral responsibility to help poorer nations overcome pollution problems; they must also end the terrible abuse of dumping toxic chemicals in poorer countries. The Vatican notes, too, that the right to a safe environment is increasingly recognized as a right that should be included in an updated Charter of Human Rights.

Church documents identify many factors contributing to ecological degradation, including war, population growth, industrial pollution, poverty, and the maldistribution of the goods of creation. They devote the most attention to the importance of environmentally and socially sustainable patterns of consumption and development, pointedly warning that richer nations must find ways to simplify their lifestyles and to share with all peoples and future generations.

5

Future Challenges

Pope Leo XIII in *Rerum Novarum* began the modern tradition of Catholic social teaching to address the new situation created by the Industrial Revolution. As this new century begins, the situation has changed again, indeed is in something of a constant flux. Catholic social teaching, to be faithful to its tradition, must evolve to meet these new challenges to Christian living.

Consider some of the elements of the new situation.

- The industrial age has been replaced—at least in the West—by an age of information and communications, which will soon morph into something else as yet unnamed.
- The modern era has come through a period of post-modern relativism and is still searching for perspectives and processes to give guidance and meaning to life.
- Relativizing post-modern and cross-cultural forms of consciousness and searching for meaning offers opportunities to the Church while at the same time challenging its dogmatic teachings and intellectual self-confidence.
- Genetic breakthroughs are opening the way for currently unimagined social scenarios.
- The Cold War has given way to many regional wars and the dominance of a single superpower.
- New forms of war and strategies of war are emerging in response to new technologies and the violence of the powerless—crime and terrorism.
- National sovereignty is under serious challenge from a form of globalization driven by technology and the interests of transnational corporations.
- Governments are too often captive to corporate wealth and agendas, not tending to issues of the common good while leaving people frus-

trated, alienated and feeling powerless.

- The institutional and moral authority of church leaders and church governance structures themselves are under stress from internal scandals, the rise of Catholic fundamentalism and clericalism.
- Catholic social teaching, which stresses the moral obligation to develop open, transparent, participatory and accountable governance structures at all levels of human society, is too often undermined by the Church's own governance structure and practice.
- Cultures have become more aware of each other and enriched by each other, but they also now compete on the uneven playing fields of the global media and international multilateral institutions.
- The dramatic gap between the comfortable, wealthy minority and the vast majority trapped in dehumanizing poverty continues to grow and stir social unrest.
- Flows of immigrants and refugees are growing to historic proportions.
- Social movements, energized by deteriorating social conditions and facilitated by global communications networks, have become a major force as a voice declaring that a different world is possible.
- The changing consciousness of the rights, talents and roles of women has spread to every nation around the planet as a transformative social force.
- The emergence of an educated and active laity and new forms of organization among them are opening new possibilities for church organization and teaching processes.
- China and India are slowly emerging as major forces on the world stage, bringing with them Eastern perspectives, cultural values, world religions and philosophical systems of thought.
- The planetary ecology is showing stress from the impact of human activities, and the human community is becoming more aware of the limits that imposes on development.

The challenges for the future of Catholic social teaching raised by these trends are clearly many and great. What shape the response will take is not yet very clear. Is it necessary to re-frame Catholic social teaching in some fundamental way? Must new principles be developed? Are the current principles capable of adaptation to the new situations? Must new processes for developing and promoting Catholic social teaching evolve? The answer to all these questions is probably "Yes, to some extent."

PROMISING BEGINNINGS

Much of the work of answering them substantively lies ahead, but some important beginnings have been made. Since Pope John XXIII in the early

1960s, Popes and official Catholic teaching bodies have been noting the necessity of some form of global government organized according to the principle of subsidiarity, serving authentic human development and the global common good. Institutions of international governance are being created, but their current configuration serves a trade-driven economic ideology that is consolidating wealth and aggravating poverty, eroding human rights protections, overriding legitimate responsibilities of local and national governments, and failing to protect the global commons.

Catholic social teaching needs to address these injustices as well as corruption at all levels and to develop more fully principles of good governance and subsidiarity, articulating the Church's vision for healthy global government properly related to national and local governments. That vision will have to have an important role for the new global phenomenon ("signs of the times") of vocal and articulate social movements. Gathering in massive convocations and employing a growing array of creative advocacy strategies, these movements express rising global discontent with poverty and corrupt governance, give voice to profound and frustrated human aspirations, and give preliminary shape to a more just and viable alternative vision.

Another promising beginning in the economic arena is Pope John Paul II's effort to address the nature of work, the vocation of workers, and the role of corporations in society in his 1981 encyclical *On Human Work (Laborem Exercens)*. His seminal ideas need to be elaborated to deal more effectively with the tensions and trade-offs business people must face when competition has become global and technology can replace workers and reduce the available employment in society. In addition, Catholic social teaching needs to address explicitly the problem of corporations that have grown beyond the regulatory control of nation states and search for ways to guarantee that their energies and activities serve the common good.

In *One Hundred Years (Centesimus Annus)*, John Paul II began to address the issues raised by the emergence of a single global superpower promoting a single dominant economic system. As already noted, Popes Leo XIII and Paul VI both insisted that agreements between unequal parties are not necessarily just simply because the parties have consented to them. The political dynamics are very complex when power, influence and wealth are unevenly distributed. Coercion by the stronger party is too often an irresistible temptation. How is it possible to develop an international economic and political system that deals with these imbalances justly and peacefully?

If the world community fails in this effort, social unrest, conflict and war will continue to increase. The Church's teaching in the areas of peacemaking and war also needs renewal and reshaping. Institutions, policies and processes of peacemaking must be envisioned and developed for the world community. The criteria for evaluating the justifications for war and the traditional principles guiding the waging of war need thorough reconsideration in the light of the globalized context, the imbalances of power, the presence of international governance institutions, terrorism, so-called "smart weapons," preemptive security strategies, the tactics of urban warfare that target essential civilian infrastructures, the increasing manipulation and control of information and public opinion in the service of military ends, and more. The economic and social costs of war and the arms trade need much more attention.

Two more important stepping stones into the future are spelled out in *One Hundred Years (Centesimus Annus)*. There, Pope John Paul II emphasized the importance of the "social mortgage" that sets limits to the right of private property. And he put forward the firm position that anything essential for human survival and development must not be controlled exclusively by market forces. These are critical principles for dealing with the strong political pressure to patent essential medications and foodstuffs and to privatize essential public services. They suggest that intellectual property rights must yield when faced with basic human survival needs. These principles need further elaboration and widespread dissemination.

In general, issues of the common good, social reproduction and the global commons need more explicit and careful attention. The current dominant processes of globalization serve a competitive, market-driven approach to economic development. In this approach, the essential processes for nurturing family life and building communities (social reproduction) are overlooked, undervalued and relegated to private life, generally to be the primary responsibility of women. And the rich resources of the global commons are being monopolized by a small wealthy and aggressive segment of the human community.

Pope John Paul II has called for a different form of globalization, a globalization of solidarity. But the Church still needs to elaborate its vision of global solidarity, lay out the framework for alternative, more just approaches and institutions, and provide a clear, sophisticated and prophetic challenge to the injustices of the current processes.

The pope has been outspoken frequently about one of these injustices: the coexistence of dire poverty and "unacceptable superdevelopment." He has repeatedly challenged people living with plenty to review their lifestyles in the face of devastating poverty and the call to global solidarity.

The responses of individuals and local churches to this challenge are often comfortably generous. The responses of nations and whole peoples have been much less positive. And on the levels of policy change and structural transformation, there is a long history of resistance to the challenge.

This is true of a broad range of issues and positions put forward by Catholic social teaching. One of the most important challenges confronting the Church today is how to make its message more compelling and get its vision and teaching effectively translated into personal and institutional living.

FOUNDATIONAL CHALLENGES

At a more radical level, modifying and strengthening the foundations—and therefore the effective authority—of the social teaching may help the Church meet that challenge. That will require at least three fundamental changes to be undertaken.

First, the Church must respond to the insightful feminist critique that the anthropology upon which its social teaching is built is flawed. It defines women's "nature" and social roles in discredited, stereotypical Western cultural categories. It implicitly, perhaps unconsciously, treats the male experience as normatively human. It assumes a dualism (body/soul, flesh/spirit) that distorts its social judgments. Only by correcting this set of biases will Catholic social teaching become able to lay out a fully adequate and life-giving vision of social solidarity.

Second, the Church must acknowledge that its social teaching thus far has been dominated by Western European Christian cultural perspectives, values, principles and social constructs. The Church identifies itself as a world church, incarnate in all the world's cultures, captive of none. It is clear in today's globalizing world, therefore, that cross-cultural and interreligious dialogue must shape future Church teaching on the social order. The Church must challenge the imposition of Western forms of property and governance at the global level by wealthy and powerful governments. Those institutions and policies risk facilitating continued Western global dominance. The Church's option for the poor and excluded also calls it to seek out and honor the social visions and cultural values of indigenous and other marginalized peoples and to promote them in the formation of the global social order.

Third, to achieve these two important foundational reorientations, the Church must develop its social teaching in more open, participatory and accountable ways. Its methodologies must become more inclusive, building upon the full range of social, cultural, economic and political experience and social judgment of the human community. Teaching intended for the universal Church needs to become more visibly the result of listening to the experience of all the local and regional churches. Far from lessening the authority of the teaching, as some in the Church fear, this approach will enhance the power of the teaching and increase its acceptance. The experience of the U.S. Church in developing its pastoral letters on peace and the economy has pointed in that direction.

Catholic social thought and teaching comprise a rich and textured faith response to the social challenges of contemporary life. It is a living tradition, evolving as people attempt to work out together ways to live their faith in meaningful ways. The outlines in this book are a sketchy introduction intended to break open for a wide audience what has been hidden, secret for too long. If it is successful, it will generate greater interest in this valuable tradition and, more importantly, it will help its readers embrace wiser, more faithful forms of Christian living.

PART TWO

DOCUMENTS TO THE UNIVERSAL CHURCH

INTRODUCTION

In this edition, we have reorganized the document outlines into two sections. The first contains documents issued by the Vatican to the whole Church. Most of these documents are encyclicals, the most formal and authoritative form of papal teaching. A few have come from the Pontifical Council for Justice and Peace or other Vatican offices, and one is the product of an international synod of bishops.

These documents are addressed *to* the universal Church. They address emerging issues of social concern to churches and peoples everywhere, applying and developing broad Christian social principles. Although almost always enriched by consultation with people in other parts of the Church in the course of their preparation, these remain papal or Vatican documents. As such, they generally reflect Western and European perspectives and values. They are intended to be received and interpreted by church communities in all cultures and nations.

The outlines in this section are summaries of some of the major documents of the Catholic Church's modern social tradition. They are designed to highlight the key points of each document and serve as a reference for further study and explanation. They are not a substitute for a thorough reading of each document. The numbers in parentheses at the end of the sentences in the outlines refer to the paragraph numbers of the text of the original documents. These may be used to locate the full development of the points made in the outline.

These documents, obviously, are not the only examples of the Church's social teaching. They were chosen because they are outstanding examples of the development of the themes of peace and justice. They provide a solid foundation upon which the Church in all its local communities can build in addressing the difficult global issues facing the human family today and into the future.

1

ON THE CONDITION OF LABOR

Rerum Novarum, Encyclical Letter of Pope Leo XIII, 1891

Major Areas of Concern
—Care for the Poor
—Rights of Workers
—Role of Private Property
—Duties of Workers and Employers
—Return to Christian Morals
—Role of Public Authority

In this encyclical Pope Leo XIII examines the situation of the poor people and workers in industrialized countries. He states several important principles that should guide the response to these people. He then articulates the role of the Church, workers and employers, and the law and public authorities in working together to build a just society. Employers are given the major role as agents for change.

HISTORICAL NOTE

The terrible exploitation and poverty of European and North American workers at the end of the nineteenth century prompted the writing of *On the Condition of Labor*. The document was inspired by the work of the Fribourg Union, a Catholic Social Action movement in Germany, and by request from the hierarchy in England, Ireland, and the United States.

A. The Situation of the Poor and Workers
1. Destitution of the masses and the wealth of a few (#1).
2. Decline of public morality (#2).
3. Workers exploited by greedy employers (#6).
4. Public authorities *not* protecting the rights of the poor (#6).

B. Guiding Principles
1. All have been created by, strive toward, and have been redeemed by God; divine grace and the goods of nature belong equally to all (#'s 11, 12, 38).
2. Natural inequalities in talents exist among people, but God has gifted all with equal dignity (#26).
3. Ability to reason is part of human nature; humans rule themselves by reason (#'s 11–12).
4. Common good is the end of civil society; all have the right to participate in society (#71).
5. True dignity resides in moral living; people of virtue will have eternal happiness (#'s 37, 42).
6. "Laws are to be obeyed only insofar as they conform with right reason and the eternal law of God" (#72).
7. National wealth originates from the labor of workers (#51).
8. All have the right to own private property (Leo criticized socialism as inherently unjust for violating this right); private property must serve the common good (#'s 2, 9, 10, 15, 23, 36, 55).
9. People have the right to the fruits of their labor but should use them to benefit all (#14).
10. Labor is necessary and there will be hardships in life (#62).
11. Wealth is a hindrance to eternal life (#34).
12. Just ownership is distinct from just use of property (#35).

C. Role of the Church
1. The Church has the right to speak out; social matters affect religion and morality (#24).
2. Through use of Gospel principles the Church can help reconcile and unify classes (#'s 25, 33, 41).
3. The Church can educate people to act justly (#'s 40, 42).

D. Rights and Duties of Workers/Poor and Employers/Wealthy of Society
1. Workers/Poor
   a. Rights: private property, poor must be cared for, possess fruits of their labor, rights of families, freedom of action, right to work, just wage (enough to support a family), join

workers' associations (which uphold religious values) (#'s 5, 9, 48, 55, 62, 63, 69).

    b. Duties: to work well, not to harm property of employer, to refrain from violence and rioting, to be thrifty (#30).

2. Employers/Wealthy
    a. Rights: private property, no crushing taxes, private societies (#'s 8, 9, 36, 72).
    b. Duties: not to treat workers as slaves, uphold dignity of workers, let workers attend to their religious and family obligations, not to impose more work than a person's strength can endure, pay a just wage, not to tamper with worker's savings, to give to the poor after needs have been met (#'s 31–32).

E. Role of Public Authority and Law in Society

1. Defend and foster the rights of families (#21).
2. Support the common good (#4).
3. Safeguard well-being and rights of non-owning workers (#49).
4. Intervene when necessary to prevent harm to individuals or the common good (#52).
5. Give special consideration to the rights of the poor (#'s 51, 54).
6. Uphold rights of private property and enable all to possess private property (#'s 55, 65).
7. Uphold the rights of associations and the religious rights of people (#69).

2

THE RECONSTRUCTION
OF THE SOCIAL ORDER

Quadragesimo Anno, Encyclical Letter of Pope Pius XI, 1931

Major Areas of Concern
—Role of the Church
—Responsible Ownership
—Labor and Capital
—Public Authority
—Just Social Order
—Capitalism and Socialism

Pope Pius XI covers three major areas in this encyclical. First, he describes the impact of Leo XIII's *On the Condition of Labor* on the Church, civil authorities, and other concerned parties. Secondly, Pius clarifies and develops the social and economic doctrine contained in *On the Condition of Labor*. He articulates a positive role for the Church in economic and social affairs and affirms the social responsibility of ownership. He advocates a unity between capital and labor and urges the uplifting of the poor and a reform of the social order based on a reestablishment of vocational groups. Finally, Pius treats the abuses of capitalism and socialism and calls for the moral renovation of society coupled with action for justice based on love.

HISTORICAL NOTE

The Reconstruction of the Social Order commemorates the fortieth anniversary of *On the Condition of Labor*. Pius wrote and issued this encyclical during a time when major depression was shaking the economic and social foundations in society worldwide. He strongly criticized the abuses of both capitalism and communism and attempted to update Catholic social teaching to reflect changed conditions. He broadened the Church's concern for poor workers to encompass the structures which oppress them.

Part One: Impact of *On the Condition of Labor*

I. On the Church

A. Doctrine
1. Encouraged adaptability to changing conditions (#18).
2. Committed many priests and lay people to the Church's social teaching (#19).
3. Inspired a truly Christian social science (#20).
4. Taught in seminars and universities (#20).
5. Had influence outside the Church (#21).

B. Practical Application
1. Effort to help lower classes (#23).
2. Influenced education and culture (#23).
3. Works of charity multiplied (#24).
4. Inspired institutions for mutual support (#24).

II. On Civil Authorities

1. Defined positive role: to protect law and order and to promote public well-being (#25).
2. Government must have a special regard for the infirm and needy (#25).
3. Leaders became more conscious of their obligations to promote social policy (#26).
4. Laws and programs for the poor were begun (#28).

III. On Other Concerned Parties

A. Unions
1. Confirmed their mission (#31).
2. Clergy and laity helped create them (#33).
3. Unions have flourished (#33).
4. Leo XIII's counsels should be adapted to different situations (#34).

B. Other
   1. Associations of employers did not meet with much success (#38).
   2. Leo XIII drew his inspiration from the Gospel (#39).

Part Two: Social and Economic Doctrine

A. **Role of the Church (#41)**
   1. Church has a right and duty to deal with these issues.
   2. It is a "God given task."
   3. Church must pass judgment on social and economic questions as they affect moral issues.
B. **Property Rights**
   1. Two-fold aspect of ownership: individual and social (concerns for the common good) (#45).
   2. Double danger: individualism and collectivism (#46).
   3. Right of property must be distinguished from its use (#47).
   4. To destroy the individual character of ownership is a grievous error (#48).
   5. Right of ownership is not absolute (#49).
   6. Function of government: to define in detail the duties of ownership (#49).
   7. Two uses of superfluous income:
      a. charity (#50);
      b. to create employment (#51).
C. **Capital and Labor**
   1. Only by the labor of working people does the state grow rich (#53).
   2. Labor and capital need each other (#53).
   3. In history, capital claimed all the products and profits and left the barest minimum to labor (#54).
   4. Unjust claim of labor: all products and profit belong to working people (#55).
   5. Advocates a just distribution of wealth to serve the common good (#56).
D. **Uplifting the Proletariat**
   1. Uplifting the proletariat is the main objective (#59).
   2. The situation of workers has improved in Western nations (#59).
   3. But the situation has deteriorated in other parts of the world (#60).
   4. Condition of rural laborers is extremely depressed (#60).
   5. Working people should be sufficiently supplied with fruits of production (#61).

6. A just wage should be paid so people can acquire moderate ownership (#63).
7. The idea of a wage contract is not necessarily unjust (#64).
8. Wage contract should be modified by a contract of partnerships (#65).
9. Demand of social justice: wages should support families (#71).
10. Women and children should not be abused in the work world (#71).
11. Public authorities can help businesses pay a just wage (#73).
12. Opportunities must be provided to those willing to work (#74).

E. **Reform of Social Order**
   1. This is primarily the State's responsibility (#78).
   2. Principles of subsidiarity: activity that can be performed by a more decentralized entity should be (#'s 79–80).
   3. Primary duty of the State: to abolish conflict and promote harmony between classes (#81).
   4. Importance of vocational groups: common effort for the common good (#84).
   5. Proper ordering of economic affairs cannot be left to free enterprise alone (#88).
   6. Economic supremacy has replaced free competition (#88).
   7. Economic institutions must be imbued with a spirit of justice (#89).
   8. Calls for international economic cooperation (#89).
   9. Supports public intervention in labor-management disputes (#93).

Part Three: Capitalism and Socialism

A. **Changes in Capitalism**
   1. Economic concentration has led to a struggle for domination (#105).
   2. Free competition has ended (#109).
   3. State has become a "slave" serving greed (#109).
   4. Economic imperialism thrives (#109).
B. **Changes in Socialism**
   1. Divided into two camps (#111).
   2. Communism supports violence and the abolition of private ownership (#112).
   3. Socialism condemns the resort to physical force and moderates the prohibition on private property (#113).

C. Remedies

1. No possibility of a compromise between Christianity and Socialism (#116).
2. Socialism perceives humans in a way alien to Christian truth (#118).
3. Social reconstruction needs a return to Christian spirit and Gospel principles (#136).
4. Love and charity must reinforce justice (#137).

3

CHRISTIANITY AND SOCIAL PROGRESS

Mater et Magistra, Encyclical Letter of Pope John XXIII, 1961

Major Areas of Concern
—Just Remuneration
—Subsidiarity
—Agriculture
—Economic Development
—Role of the Church
—International Cooperation
—Socialization

Pope John XXIII begins this encyclical by reviewing the major points of *On the Condition of Labor* and *The Reconstruction of the Social Order*. He notes that new political, social, and economic developments have necessitated *Christianity and Social Progress*. He confirms previous papal teaching on the value of private initiative, just remuneration for work, and the social function of private property. John XXIII then treats the questions of agriculture and aid to developing countries. He urges a reconstruction of social relationships according to the principles of Catholic social teaching and states the responsibility of individual Christians to work for a more just world.

HISTORICAL NOTE

Pope John XXIII issued *Christianity and Social Progress* in response to the severe imbalances between the rich and the poor which exist in the world. The encyclical commemorates the seventieth anniversary of Leo XIII's *On the Condition of Labor*. John XXIII "internationalizes" the Catholic social teaching by treating, for the first time, the situation of countries which are not fully industrialized. He articulates an important role for the laity in applying the Church's social teachings in the world.

I. New Developments

A. Economic and Scientific (#47)
1. Discovery of atomic energy.
2. Synthetic products and automation.
3. Conquest of outer space.
4. New speed of transportation.
5. Improvements in communications.

B. Social (#48)
1. Insurance and social security.
2. Improvements in education.
3. Increased social mobility.
4. Pronounced imbalances between more developed and less developed areas.

C. Political (#49)
1. Increased participation.
2. Less colonization.
3. More public intervention.

II. Development of Social Teaching

A. Private Initiative
1. First priority to private initiative (#51).
2. Supports principle of "subsidiarity" (#53).
3. Public authorities can intervene to reduce economic imbalances (#54).
4. Balance between public and private initiative (#55).
5. Socialization: interdependent social relationships with positive and negative consequences created by new developments (#'s 59–67).

B. Just Remuneration for Work

1. Families need appropriate wage to live in dignity (#68).
2. World imbalance: too much money spent on national prestige and armaments (#69).
3. Economic development must correspond to social development (#73).
4. Economic prosperity: the just and proper distribution of goods (#74).
5. Workers should share in running of companies (management, profits, ownership) (#75).
6. Requirements for common good for nations (#79):
   a. create employment;
   b. care for less privileged;
   c. provide for the future.

C. Justice and Productive Institutions

1. Foster small and intermediary holdings (#84).
2. Encourage family-type ownership (#85).
3. Alleviate imbalances (#84).
4. All should work for the common good (#96).

D. Private Property

1. Confirms rights to private property (#109).
2. Encourages widespread ownership (#115).
3. State can own means of production (but affirms subsidiarity) (#117).
4. Social responsibility: a function of private property (#119).

III. New Aspects of the Social Question

A. Agriculture

1. Agriculture is a depressed sector; imbalances between it and industry exist (#123).
2. Church calls for services for rural areas and orderly economic development (#127).
3. Appropriate economic policy includes capital at suitable prices, price protection, social security, and strengthening farm income (#'s 131–143).
4. Principal agent for improvement should be rural workers, who have dignity from God (#144).

B. Aid to Less Developed Areas

1. Need for competent administration and economic policies (#150).
2. Citizens in less developed areas are chiefly responsible for their own development and need to respect dignity and subsidiarity (#151).

C. **Justice between Nations Differing in Development**
1. Peace is more difficult as imbalances persist (#157).
2. Duty of countries to help the poor and unfortunate (#157).
3. Need to establish an effective program of emergency assistance (#161).
4. Private enterprises and societies need to be more generous in cooperation (#165).
5. Industrial countries need to respect the culture of developing countries; aid should be offered without the intent to dominate (#'s 170, 172).

D. **Role of the Church**
1. Individual Christians must advance civil institutions and human dignity and foster a unity between peoples (#179).
2. Many Catholics are already involved in these efforts (#182).

E. **Population Increase and Development**
1. Humankind has an inexhaustible productive capacity (#189).
2. Humans should not resort to means of population control beneath human dignity (#199).

F. **International Cooperation**
1. Relationships are interdependent; cooperation and mutual assistance are needed (#200).
2. Cause of distrust is failure to agree on laws of justice; armaments are a symptom of this distrust (#203).

IV. **Reconstruction of Social Relationships**

A. **Incomplete Philosophies of Life**
1. Many philosophies do not encompass the entire human person or respect human dignity (#'s 213–214).
2. It is folly to establish a temporal order without God as a foundation (#217).

B. **Catholic Social Teaching (CST)**
1. Individuals are the foundation, cause, and end of all social institutions (#219).
2. CST cannot be separated from Church teachings on life and should be taught at all levels and in the media (#'s 222–223).
3. Catholics should be reared on CST and conform their social and economic behavior to CST principles (#228).
4. Applying CST in the world is difficult (#229).
5. How to apply CST (task for laity) (#'s 236–241):
   a. examine situation (observe);
   b. evaluate it with respect to CST (judge);
   c. decide how to act (act).

C. Conclusion

1. Industrial life can deform values and depart from human dignity (#242).
2. Church needs to renew its dedication in seeking to establish the Kingdom in temporal affairs (#254).

4

PEACE ON EARTH

Pacem in Terris, Encyclical Letter of Pope John XXIII, 1963

Major Areas of Concern
—Rights and Duties
—Role of Public Authorities
—Common Good
—Christian World Order
—International Relations
—Disarmament

In *Peace on Earth*, Pope John XXIII contends that peace can be established only if the social order set down by God is fully observed. Relying extensively on reason and the natural law tradition, John XXIII sketches a list of rights and duties to be followed by individuals, public authorities, national governments, and the world community. Peace needs to be based on an order "founded on truth, built according to justice, vivified and integrated by charity, and put into practice in freedom."

HISTORICAL NOTE

Written during the first year of Vatican II, *Peace on Earth* was the first encyclical addressed to "all people of good will." Issued shortly after the

Cuban Missile Crisis in 1962 and the erection of the Berlin Wall, this document spoke to a world aware of the dangers of nuclear war. Its optimistic tone and development of a philosophy of rights made a significant impression on Catholics and non-Catholics alike.

I. Order between People

Every human is a person, endowed with intelligence and free will, who has universal and inviolable rights and duties (#9).

A. Rights

1. Rights to life and worthy standard of living, including rights to proper development of life and to basic security (#11).
2. Rights of cultural and moral values, including freedom to search for and express opinions, freedom of information, and right to education (#'s 12–13).
3. Rights to religion and conscience (#14).
4. Rights to choose one's state in life, including rights to establish a family and pursue a religious vocation (#'s 15–16).
5. Economic rights, including right to work, to a just and sufficient wage, and to hold private property (#'s 18–22).
6. Rights of meeting and association (#23).
7. Right to emigrate and immigrate (#25).
8. Political rights, including right to participate in public affairs and juridical protection of rights (#'s 26–27).

B. Duties

1. To acknowledge and respect rights of others (#30).
2. To collaborate mutually (#31).
3. To act for others responsibly (#39).
4. To preserve life and live it becomingly (#42).

C. Signs of the Times

1. Working classes have gradually gained ground in economic and social affairs (#40).
2. Women are participating in public life (#41).
3. All nations are becoming independent (#42).

II. Relations between Individuals and Public Authorities in a Single State

A. Nature of Authority

1. Authority is necessary for the proper functioning of society (#46).
2. It derives its force from the moral order which has God for its end (#47).
3. A state which uses, as its chief means, punishments and rewards cannot effectively promote the common good (#48).

    4. A state cannot oblige in matters of conscience (#49).

    5. A command contrary to God's will is not binding (#51).

B. Characteristics of Common Good

    1. Human person must be considered (#55).

    2. All members of the state share in common good (#56).

    3. More attention must be given to the less fortunate members of society (#56).

    4. State must promote material and spiritual welfare of citizens (#57).

C. Civil Authority

    1. Chief concern should be to ensure the common good (#59).

    2. Coordinates social relations in a way that allows people to exercise their rights and duties peacefully (#60).

    3. A three-fold division of powers—legislative, executive, and judicial—is recommended for public authorities (#68).

    4. Often a prudent and thoughtful juridical system seems inadequate for society's needs (#71).

    5. Three requisites for good government:

       a. charter of human rights (#75);

       b. written constitution (#76);

       c. relations between governed and government in terms of rights and duties (#77).

III. Relations between States

A. In Truth

    1. Elimination of racism (#86).

    2. Right to self-development (#86).

    3. Obligation of mutual assistance (#87).

    4. Objective use of media (#90).

B. In Justice

    1. Recognition of mutual rights and duties (#91).

    2. Improvement of the situation of ethnic minorities (#96).

C. Active Solidarity

    1. Promote by civil authority the common good of the entire human family (#98).

    2. Fostering of friendly relations in all fields (#100).

    3. Reduction in imbalances of goods and capital in the world (#101).

    4. Right of political refugees to migrate (#106).

    5. Arms race:

       a. deprives less developed countries of social and economic progress (#109);

      b. creates a climate of fear (#111);

      c. "Justice, then, right reason, and consideration for human dignity and life demand that the arms race cease" (#112);

      d. peace consists in mutual trust (#114).

D. In Liberty

1. Relations based on freedom; responsibility and enterprise encouraged (#120).
2. Respect by the wealthy nations of the value in giving aid without seeking dominance (#125).

IV. Relations of People and of Political Communities with the World Community

1. Individual countries cannot seek their own interests and develop in isolation given modern conditions of interdependence (#131).
2. Under present circumstances, the structures and forms of national governments are inadequate to promote the universal common good (#135).
3. Public authority must have the means to promote the common good (#136).
4. Need public authority to operate in an effective manner on a world-wide matter (#137).
5. The United Nations should be fostered (#145).

V. Pastoral Exhortations

1. People should take an active role in public life and organizations and influence them from within (#147).
2. Humans should carry on temporal activities "as acts within the moral order" (#150).
3. A unity between faith and action is needed; solid Christian education will help achieve this unity (#'s 152–153).
4. Distinguish between false philosophical ideas and movements deriving from them (#159).
5. Christians need prudence in determining when to collaborate with non-Christians in social and economic affairs (#160).
6. "Peace will be but an empty sounding word unless it is founded on the order which the present document has outlined in confident hope: an order founded on truth, built according to justice, vivified and integrated by charity, and put into practice in freedom" (#167).

5

THE CHURCH IN THE
MODERN WORLD

Gaudium et Spes, Second Vatican Council, 1965

Major Areas of Concern
—Human Dignity
—Common Good
—"Signs of the Times"
—Public Responsibility
—Respect for Families
—Right of Culture
—Justice and Development
—Peace

Vatican II's *The Church in the Modern World* is seen by many to be the most important document in the Church's social tradition. It announces the duty of the People of God to scrutinize the "signs of the times" in light of the Gospel. In doing so, it finds that change characterizes the world. These technological and social changes provide both wonderful opportunities and worrisome difficulties for the spread of the Gospel. The Church's duty in the world is to work for the enhancement of human dignity and the common good.

HISTORICAL NOTE

This document represents the opinion of the overwhelming majority of the world's Bishops. Originally, the material contained here was not scheduled to be considered separately by the Council. Cardinal Joseph Suenens of Belgium, however, intervened at the end of the first session to urge consideration of issues more "external" to the Church than the role of Bishops or the use of vernacular in the liturgy. The document is the product of a commission and was altered by a 2,300 member deliberative assembly. In final form, it represents a significant break from the rigid traditionalism of the Council's preparatory commission.

Introduction

    A. The "joys and hopes, sorrows and anxieties" of the people of the world are the concerns of the People of God (#1).
    B. Church's duty: to scrutinize the "signs of the times" (#4).
        1. Technological changes have caused social changes (#5).
        2. These changes have affected everybody—individuals, families, communities, and nations—with both good and bad results (#'s 6–7).
        3. Conflicting forces have ensued: tremendous wealth and abject poverty, great freedom and psychological slavery (#9).
        4. Conviction has grown that humanity can establish a political order that will serve human dignity (#9).

Part One: The Church and Humanity's Calling

I. Human Dignity

    A. Nature of Human
        1. Created in God's image (free and intelligent), and as a social being (#12).
        2. Split within self: inclination toward good and evil (#13).
        3. Dignity depends on freedom to obey one's conscience (#16).
    B. Christianity and Atheism
        1. Atheism: a serious concern, impeding the liberation of the complete person and antagonistic toward religion (#19).
        2. But recognition of God is in no way hostile to human dignity (#21).
        3. A living faith, activating people to justice and love, is needed to overcome suspicion of religion (#21).

    4. Church calls all to work to better the world; this work corresponds to the work of the human heart (#21).

C. Human Community

    1. Technological changes have created interdependence without fostering interpersonal relationships (#23).

    2. Advancement of individuals and society depends on everyone (#25).

    3. All must work for the common good (#26).

    4. Everything necessary for a truly human life must be made available for us (#26).

    5. Scripture mandates love of neighbor; every person is our neighbor; active love is necessary (#28).

    6. Jesus calls us God's children so we should treat each other as sisters and brothers (#32).

D. The Church in the Modern World

    1. The Church and humanity experience the same earthly situation (#40).

    2. History, science, and culture reveal the true nature of the human person (#41).

    3. The Church is not bound to any particular political, economic, or social system (#42).

    4. The Church needs to purify itself continually (#43).

    5. Individual Christians need to penetrate the world with a Christian spirit and witness to Jesus in the midst of human society (#43).

    6. The Church can be helped by the world in preparing the ground for the Gospel (#44).

    7. The Church's mission, part saving and part eschatological, begins in this world; Jesus is Lord of history (#45).

Part Two: Special Areas of Concern

I. Marriage and the Family

    1. Families are the foundation of society (#47).

    2. Destructive to marriage are: divorce, free love, excessive self-love, polygamy, worship of pleasure, certain modern economic-social-political conditions, overpopulation (#47).

    3. Marriage is intended for the procreation and education of children and a whole manner and communion of life (#50).

    4. Responsible parenthood is advocated (#50).

    5. From the moment of conception, life must be regarded with sacred care (#51).

    6. The healthy condition of individuals and society depends on stable families (#52).

II. The Development of Culture

A. Circumstances of Culture

1. Changes in technology have created fresh avenues for the diffusion of culture (#54).
2. A new humanism has dawned and an individual is defined by his/her responsibilities to the world (#55).
3. Culture must evolve so as to foster the development of the whole person (#56).

B. Principles of Cultural Development

1. The quest for heaven should inspire Christians to build a more human world on earth (#57).
2. Danger exists that humans may rely on modern discoveries and stop searching for higher realities (#57).
3. God speaks to the various cultures (#58).
4. Church, in ways that respect its own tradition, should use modes of culture to spread the Gospel (#58).
5. The Good News renews and advances culture (#58).
6. Culture needs freedom in which to develop (#59).

C. Cultural Duties of Christians

1. Strenuous work is needed in economic and political fields to liberate people from ignorance (#60).
2. Everyone has a right to culture, thought, and expression (#60).
3. Women should participate in cultural life (#60).
4. Development of the whole person should be fostered (#61).
5. Christian thinking should be expressed in ways consistent with culture (#62).

III. Socio-Economic Life

A. Basic Principles

1. Human beings are "the source, the center, and the purpose of all socio-economic life" (#63).
2. Fundamental imbalances between wealth and poverty exist in today's world (#63).

B. Economic Development

1. Technological progress which serves the whole person must be fostered (#64).
2. Progress must be controlled by humanity (#65).
3. Justice necessitates a quick removal of economic inequities (#66).

C. Economic Life

1. Human labor is superior to other elements of economic life; economic activity detrimental to the worker is wrong and inhuman (#67).

2. Workers should participate in running an enterprise (#67).
3. God intended the earth for everyone; private property should benefit all (#67).
4. All have a right to goods sufficient for themselves and their families (#69).
5. Distribution of goods should be directed toward employment (#70).
6. Public authorities can guard against those misuses of private property which hurt the common good (#71).
7. Genuine sharing of goods is called for (#71).

IV. Political Community

1. Modern changes have increased the awareness of human dignity and the desire to establish a just political-juridical order (#73).
2. Public authorities (and individual citizens) should work for the common good (#74).
3. Church and political community (#76):
   a. both serve the vocation of humans;
   b. Church has the right to pass moral judgments when human rights are at stake;
   c. Church should use the means of the Gospel to fulfill its mission.

V. Peace

A. Basic Principles

1. With modern weapons, humanity is in a crisis situation (#77).
2. Most noble meaning of "peace"—based on love, harmony, trust, and justice—should be fostered (#78).

B. Avoidance of War

1. Non-violence and conscientious objection are legitimate (#79).
2. Just defense is permissible, but not wars of subjugation (#79).
3. Participation in armed services is allowed, but not blind obedience to orders (#79).
4. With new weapons, a new evaluation of war is needed (#80).
5. Arms race is not the way to build peace; it can actually foster wars and it injures the poor (#81).
6. No act of war at population centers is permissible (#81).
7. Deterrence "is not a safe way to preserve steady peace" (#81).
8. Everyone has responsibility to work for disarmament (#82).

C. Building Up the International Community

1. Causes of dissension, especially injustices, need to be eliminated (#83).
2. Greater international cooperation demands the establishment of an international organization corresponding to modern obligations (#'s 84–85).
3. Development of whole person is to be fostered (#86).
4. Ecumenical cooperation is needed to achieve justice (#88).
5. Church must be present to injustice (#89).

6

THE DEVELOPMENT OF PEOPLES

Populorum Progressio, Encyclical Letter of Pope Paul VI, 1967

> **Major Areas of Concern**
> —Human Aspirations
> —Structural Injustice
> —Church and Development
> —New Humanism
> —Common Good
> —Economic Planning
> —International Trade
> —Peace

In *The Development of Peoples,* Pope Paul VI speaks to the challenge of development. He explores the nature of poverty and the conflicts it produces. He articulates the role of the Church in the process of development and sketches a Christian vision of development. The Pope calls for urgent action which respects the universal purpose of created things. He advocates economic planning and aid to promote development. Paul VI urges equity in trade relations as well as universal charity. He concludes by terming "development" the new name for peace and exhorts all Christians to strive for justice.

HISTORICAL NOTE

In this encyclical, Paul VI enlarges the scope of Leo XIII's treatment of the struggle between the rich and poor classes to encompass the conflict between rich and poor nations. *The Development of Peoples* is the first encyclical devoted entirely to the international development issue. The Pope stresses the economic sources of war and highlights economic justice as the basis of peace. More so than any of his predecessors, Paul VI explicitly criticizes basic tenets of capitalism, including the profit motive and the unrestricted right of private property.

I. Humanity's Complete Development

A. The Data of the Problem
    1. Human aspirations include (#6):
        a. freedom from misery;
        b. food security;
        c. responsibility without oppression;
        d. better education.
    2. The means inherited from the past are not lacking but are insufficient for the present situation (#7).
    3. Social conflicts now have a worldwide dimension (#9).
    4. Structures have not adapted themselves to the new conditions (#10).

B. The Church and Development
    1. Responding to the teaching of Jesus, the Church must foster human progress (#12).
    2. World demands action based on a vision of the economic, social, cultural, and spiritual aspects of the situation (#13).
    3. The Church was "founded to establish on earth the Kingdom of Heaven" (#13).
    4. Development cannot be limited to economic growth but looks to total human potential (#14).
    5. People have a right and a duty to develop themselves; as beings with a spiritual dimension, people should orient their lives to God, creating a transcendent humanism (#'s 15–16).
    6. Each person is a member of society (#17).
    7. Work is a necessity but greed must be avoided (#18).
    8. Avarice is the most blatant form of moral underdevelopment (#19).
    9. A new humanism embracing higher values of love, friendship, prayer, and contemplation is needed for a full and authentic development (#20).

C. Action to Be Undertaken
  1. Universal purpose of created things:
      a. God intends the earth and its goods for use by everyone; all other rights must be subordinated to this (#22).
      b. Private property is not an absolute and unconditional right, but must be exercised for the common good; public authority must ensure this, and the common good sometimes requires expropriation (#'s 23–24).
  2. Industrialization.
      a. Industry is necessary for economic growth and progress (#25).
      b. Structures of capitalism—profit, competition, and absolute private ownership—are "unfortunate" (#26).
      c. Industrialization can be separated from the capitalistic system (#26).
  3. Urgency to the task.
      a. Too many people are suffering; disparity between the rich and poor grows (#29).
      b. With situations of injustice, recourse to violence is a grave temptation (#30).
      c. Cautions against revolutions; greater misery may result (#31).
      d. Present situation must be fought against and overcome (#32).
  4. Programs and planning.
      a. Individual initiative and free competition are not enough; public programs are necessary (#33).
      b. Public authorities must choose objectives and stimulate activity (#33).
      c. Service of humanity is the aim of development (#34).
      d. Economic growth depends on social progress; better education is needed (#35).
      e. Christians should not subscribe to doctrines based on materialistic and atheistic philosophies (#39).
      f. Developing nations should honor their own cultures (#40).
      g. Complete humanism is the aim of development (#42).

II. Development in Solidarity

A. Aid for the Poor
  1. The problem: hunger, malnutrition, stunted physical and mental growth (#45).
  2. Response demands generosity, sacrifice, and efforts by the rich: a solidarity that costs (#46).

3. Advanced countries should offer financial and educational assistance (#47).
4. "The superfluous wealth of rich countries should be placed at the service of poor nations" (#49).
5. Recommendations: support Food and Agriculture Organization; establish a World Fund (money from arms race to aid destitute); worldwide collaboration and dialogue (#52–54).
6. Public and private squandering of wealth is an intolerable scandal (#53).

B. **Equity in Trade Relations**
1. The problem: industrialized nations export primarily manufactured goods; developing nations raw goods; price of manufactured goods is increasing; raw materials are subject to wide price fluctuation; developing nations have great difficulty in balancing their economies (#57).
2. Free trade is no longer capable of governing international relations (#58).
3. The fundamental principles of liberalism are in question (#58).
4. *On the Condition of Labor* held that if the positions of the contracting parties are unequal, the contract is void (#59).
5. Freedom of trade is fair only if it is subject to the demands of social justice (#59).
6. Discussion and negotiation are necessary to reach equality of opportunity (#61).
7. Nationalism and racism are major obstacles of justice (#62).

C. **Universal Charity**
1. "The world is sick": lack of concern for others (#66).
2. It is the duty of people to welcome others, especially youth and migrant workers (#67).
3. Business people in developing nations should be initiators of social progress and human advancement (#70).
4. Sincere dialogue and affection are needed (#73).

D. **Development Is the New Name for Peace**
1. Peace is built daily in pursuit of God's order (#76).
2. People themselves have a prime responsibility for their own development (#77).
3. International collaboration on a worldwide scale for justice is needed (#78).
4. The hour for action is now (#80).
5. Role of lay persons: "to infuse a Christian spirit into the mentality, customs, laws and structures" of their communities and nations (#81).
6. Catholics should support development efforts generously (#81).

7. To struggle against injustice is to promote the common good (#82).
8. Peace is not the mere absence of war (#83).

7

A CALL TO ACTION

Octogesima Adveniens, Apostolic Letter of Pope Paul VI, 1971

Major Areas of Concern
—Urbanization
—Role of Local Churches
—Duties of Individual Christians
—Political Activity
—Worldwide Dimensions of Justice

Pope Paul VI begins this letter by urging greater efforts for justice and noting the duties of local churches to respond to specific situations. The Pope then discusses a wide variety of new social problems which stem from urbanization. These issues include women, youth, and the "new poor." Paul VI next treats modern aspirations and ideas, especially liberalism and Marxism. He stresses the need to ensure equality and the right of all to participate in society. He concludes this letter by encouraging all Christians to reflect on their contemporary situations, apply Gospel principles, and take political action when appropriate.

HISTORICAL NOTE

A Call to Action is an open, apostolic letter from Pope Paul VI to Cardinal Maurice Roy, president of the Pontifical Commission on Justice and Peace, to commemorate the eightieth anniversary of the publication of Pope Leo

XIII's *On the Condition of Labor.* It breaks new ground by developing a theory of the role of individual Christians and local churches in responding to situations of injustice.

A. Introduction
   1. Greater efforts for justice are needed (#2).
   2. Given the wide diversity of situations in the world, each local church has responsibility to discern and act (#4).
   3. A great variety of changes are taking place in the world (#7).

B. New Social Problems
   1. Urbanization creates a new loneliness and the possibility that humans may become slaves to their own creation (#10).
   2. Youth find dialogue increasingly difficult (#13).
   3. Women possess an equal right to participate in social, cultural, economic, and political life (#13).
   4. Workers have the right to form unions (#14).
   5. The "New Poor," created by urbanization, include the handicapped, elderly, and the marginalized (#15).
   6. Discrimination along lines of race, origin, color, culture, sex, and religion still exists (#17).
   7. Emigration is a right (#17).
   8. There is great need to create employment through effective policies of investment, education, and organization of means of production (#18).
   9. The media has both positive and negative potential (#20).
   10. People have a responsibility to protect the environment (#21).

C. Fundamental Aspirations and Ideas
   1. Equality and participation need to be ensured (#22).
   2. Legislation for justice is necessary but not enough; love sparking action for the poor is needed (#23).
   3. Preferential respect for the poor is important (#23).
   4. Political activity for a democratic society is consistent with the total vocation of humankind; humans can no longer rely only on economic activity (#25).
   5. Both Marxist and liberal ideologies alienate human beings (#26).
   6. Historical movements contain positive elements which must be discerned (#30).
   7. Certain features of socialism are attractive, but Christians must critique its appeal (#31).
   8. A variety of interpretations of Marxism exist but historically it has led to totalitarianism and violence (#'s 32–34).
   9. Liberalism promotes economic efficiency but distorts human nature (#35).

10. Christians need to discern carefully the options between different ideologies (#36).
11. Utopias are generally ineffective, but they provoke the imagination and activity for a better world (#37).
12. Humans have become the object of science; science lacks a total picture of humanity (#39).
13. Nature of progress is ambiguous; quality of human relations and degree of participation and responsibility are just as important as amount of goods produced (#41).

D. **Christians Face New Problems**
1. Catholic social teaching states the importance of reflecting on the changing situation of the world and applying Gospel principles to it (#42).
2. Nations need to revise their relationships to work for greater justice (#43).
3. Liberation requires changed attitudes and structures (#45).
4. The task of Christians is to create conditions for the complete good of humanity (#46).
5. Christians need to concentrate more on political rather than economic activity as a solution for contemporary problems (#46).
6. Involvement in building human solidarity is a goal of freedom (#47).

E. **Call to Action**
1. Each Christian has a personal responsibility for building up the temporal order (#48).
2. The Lord working with us is a great reason for Christian hope (#48).
3. A plurality of options for action exists (#49).
4. Christians have the task of inspiring and innovating in working for justice (#50).

8

JUSTICE IN THE WORLD

Statement of the Synod of Bishops, 1971

Major Areas of Concern
—Gospel Mandate for Justice
—Right to Development
—Justice as Christian Love
—Education for Justice
—International Action

The 1971 Synod of Bishops, in their reflection on "the mission of the People of God to further justice in the world," affirms the right to a culturally sensitive, personalized development. The Bishops teach that Gospel principles mandate justice for the liberation of all humanity as an essential expression of Christian love. The Church must witness for justice through its own lifestyle, educational activities, and international action. Structural sin is discussed.

HISTORICAL NOTE

This document illustrates the powerful influence of native leadership of the Churches of Africa, Asia, and Latin America. It is the first major example of post-Vatican II episcopal collegiality and reflects a forceful, concrete, and realistic refinement of previous papal pronouncements.

Introduction

1. Structural injustices oppress humanity and stifle freedom to operate in the world (#3).
2. The dynamism of the Gospel is consistent with the hopes of the people of today (#5).
3. "Action on behalf of justice and participation in the transformation of the world fully appear to us as a constitutive dimension of the preaching of the Gospel, or, in other words, of the Church's mission for the redemption of the human race and its liberation from every oppressive situation" (#6).

I. Justice and World Society

1. A modern paradox:
   a. forces for achieving human dignity seem strong (#7);
   b. but so do forces of division (arms race, economic injustices, lack of participation) (#9).
2. Affirms the right to development as a basic human right (#15).
3. Calls for personalization and a culturally sensitive modernization (#'s 17–19).
4. Many who suffer injustice are voiceless; the Church should speak on their behalf (#20).
5. Injustices listed: those to migrants, refugees; religious persecution; human rights violations; torture; political prisoners; anti-life; war; dishonest media; anti-family activity (#'s 21–26).
6. Dialogue with the participation of all, especially youth, is needed to correct these injustices (#28).

II. Gospel Message and Mission of Christ

A. Scriptural Sources
1. People need to listen to the Word of God to respond effectively to injustices (#29).
2. Old Testament views God as the "liberator of the oppressed and the defender of the poor" (#30).
3. Jesus gave himself for the salvation and liberation of all and associated himself with the "least" (#31).
4. St. Paul: Christian life is the faith which sparks love of and service to neighbors (#33).

B. Justice and Love
1. "Christian love of neighbor and justice cannot be separated" (#34).
2. Preaching the Gospel requires a dedication to the liberation of humanity in this world (#35).

C. Role of the Church
   1. The Gospel message gives the Church the right and duty to pro-
      claim justice on all levels and to denounce instances of injustice
      (#36).
   2. The role of the hierarchical Church is not to offer concrete
      solutions to specific problems but to promote the dignity and
      rights of each human being (#37).

III. Practice of Justice

A. Witness of the Church
   1. Anyone who ventures to preach justice should be perceived as
      being just (#40).
   2. Rights within the Church must be respected for all, especially
      women and lay people (#43).
   3. Rights include: decent wage, security, promotion, freedom of
      thought and expression, proper judicial procedures, and partic-
      ipation in decision-making process (#'s 45–46).
   4. The lifestyle of the institutional Church and all its members
      must allow it to preach the good news to the poor (#48).
B. Education for Justice
   1. In developing countries, the aim is to awaken awareness of the
      concrete situation and strategies and alternatives for change
      (#51).
   2. Family is the principal agent for this education, a continuing one
      (#54).
   3. Catholic social teaching, the basic principles of the Gospels
      applied, is the major source for justice education (#56).
   4. Liturgy and the sacraments can serve justice education (#58).
C. Cooperation between Churches in Rich and Poor Nations Is Essential for Economic and Spiritual Progress (#59).
D. Ecumenical Collaboration for Justice Is Strongly Supported (#61).
E. International Action
   1. Call for the UN Declaration of Human Rights to be ratified by
      all nations (#64).
   2. Support UN efforts to halt arms race, weapons trade, and reach
      peaceful conflict resolution (#65).
   3. Foster aims of the Second Development Decade, including fair
      prices for raw materials, opening of markets, and taxation on
      worldwide basis (#66).
   4. Concentration of power should be changed; more participation
      is needed (#67).
   5. Emphasizes the importance of UN specialized agencies in pro-
      moting justice (#68).

6. Calls for funding for responsible development (#69).
7. Wealthy nations need to be less materialistic and consume less (#70).
8. Right to development and respectful cooperation with wealthy nations are urged (#71).

IV. A Word of Hope

Christians will find the Kingdom as the fruit of their nature and efforts; God is now preparing the Kingdom (#75).

9

EVANGELIZATION IN THE MODERN WORLD

*Evangelii Nuntiandi, Apostolic
Exhortation of Pope Paul VI, 1975*

Major Areas of Concern
—Personal Conversion
—Church and Culture
—Justice and Liberation
—Universal and Individual Churches
—Gospel and Non-Christians

Evangelization in the Modern World represents Pope Paul VI's main teachings on the Church's evangelizing mission. The Pope treats the responsibility of the Church to proclaim the good news in ways that people of the twentieth century can understand. All Christians are urged to spread the Gospel. The Pope declares that combating injustices and preaching liberation constitute essential elements of evangelization.

HISTORICAL NOTE

Commemorating the tenth anniversary of the closing of the Second Vatican Council, *Evangelization in the Modern World* affirms the Council's teachings on the active role that the institutional Church and individual

Christians must play in promoting justice in the world. This apostolic exhortation was written at the request of the 1974 Synod of Bishops, which had considered the topic of evangelization but did not produce any major document on it.

Introduction

1. Objective: To make the twentieth-century Church better fitted for proclaiming the Gospel (#2).
2. The Church needs to preserve the heritage of faith and present it in the most persuasive and understandable way possible (#3).

I. Evangelizers: Christ and the Church

1. Mission of Jesus: going from town to town preaching the good news to the poorest (#6).
2. Jesus proclaimed the Kingdom of God and a salvation which is liberation from all oppression (#9).
3. A radical conversion is needed to gain the Kingdom (#10).
4. Jesus proclaimed the Kingdom with signs as well as words (#12).
5. The good news is meant for all people of all times (#13).
6. Evangelizing is "the grace and vocation proper to the Church" (#14).
7. The Church is sent by Jesus and begins by evangelizing itself (#15).

II. Evangelization: The Elements

1. Purpose: To bring the good news "into all strata of humanity," transforming it from within and making it new (#18).
2. Evangelization should affect human judgment, values, interests, thought, and way of life (#19).
3. The Gospel is independent of, but not incompatible with, culture; evangelization of culture is needed (#20).
4. Personal witness and explicit proclamation are needed for evangelization (#21).
5. Evangelization is aided by a community of believers (#23).

III. Evangelization: The Content

1. The primary message: God loves the world and, through Jesus, salvation is available to all (#'s 26–27).
2. Evangelization has a personal and social dimension involving human rights, peace, justice, development, and liberation (#29).
3. The Church must proclaim liberation (#30).

4. Humans are subject to social and economic questions; the plan of redemption includes combating injustice (#31).
5. Evangelization is a religious as well as a temporal task; Jesus must be proclaimed (#35).
6. The spiritual dimension of liberation is primary; true liberation needs to be motivated by justice and charity (#35).
7. Personal conversion is needed for structural change (#36).
8. The Church cannot accept violence (#37).
9. Religious liberty is an important human right (#39).

IV. Evangelization: The Methods

1. Preaching and the witness of an authentic Christian life are indispensable elements (#'s 41–42).
2. Homilies, catechetical instruction, and mass media also facilitate evangelization (#'s 43–45).
3. Personal contact, the sacraments, and popular piety are also necessary for effective evangelization (#'s 46–48).

V. Evangelization: The Beneficiaries

1. The good news is for everyone (#49).
2. Even today many obstacles (persecution, resistance) impede the spread of the Gospel (#50).
3. "Pre-evangelization" can be an effective aid to the spread of the good news (#51).
4. The Gospel should be proclaimed to non-Christians as well as Christians in our increasingly de-Christianized world (#53).
5. The Church needs to address atheism, humanism, and secularism (#54).
6. Non-practicing Christians should be special beneficiaries of evangelization (#56).
7. There are two kinds of "small communities": one works with the Church, bringing Christians together, and the other bitterly criticizes the Church; the former can be used for evangelization (#58).
8. Small communities need nourishment from the Word and a universal outlook (#58).

VI. Evangelization: The Workers

1. Evangelization is the mission of the Church (#60).
2. Both the universal Church and the individual churches have roles to play in the quest to spread the good news (#'s 61–62).
3. Individual churches have the task of proclaiming the Gospel in ways that people can understand (#63).

4. Evangelization needs to consider people's concrete lives (#63).
5. While faith may be translated into all expressions, its content must not be impaired (#'s 63–65).
6. There is one mission of evangelization but many different ways to achieve this goal (#66).
7. The Pope has the pre-eminent ministry of teaching the truth (#67).
8. Bishops, priests, religious, laity, young people, and families all have important roles to play in evangelization (#'s 68–72).

10

On Human Work

Laborem Exercens, Encyclical Letter of Pope John Paul II, 1981

> **Major Areas of Concern**
> —Dignity of Work
> —Capitalism and Socialism
> —Property
> —Unions
> —Employment
> —Spirituality of Work

On Human Work, Pope John Paul II's encyclical, commemorates the ninetieth anniversary of Pope Leo XIII's *On the Condition of Labor*. John Paul II affirms the dignity of work and places work at the center of the social question. The encyclical states that human beings are the proper subject of work. Work expresses and increases human dignity. The Pope stresses the priority of labor over things while criticizing systems which do not embody these principles. He supports the rights of workers and unions. John Paul II concludes by outlining a spirituality of work.

HISTORICAL NOTE

On Human Work represents a clear and succinct statement of John Paul II's thoughts on the social question. Written almost entirely by the Pope himself, this encyclical reflects statements made while he was a Polish prelate and those made during the first years of his pontificate. *On Human Work* develops and refines the Church's teachings on property and its criticism of capitalism and Marxism.

I. Introduction

1. Humans derive dignity from work even though it involves suffering and toil (#1).
2. Recent changes in the realm of work (#1):
    a. automation;
    b. increase in price of energy and raw materials;
    c. environmental awareness and respect;
    d. people claiming right to participate.
3. Role of the Church (#1):
    a. call attention to dignity of workers;
    b. condemn violations of dignity;
    c. guide changes to ensure progress.
4. Work is at the center of the social question, the key to making life more human (#2).
5. Catholic social teaching has evolved and now considers the "world" as well as the "class" perspective; the Church calls for structural transformation on a more universal scale (#2).

II. Work and Human Beings

A. Perspective on Work
1. *Genesis* states God's command to subdue the earth; work is the means to do so (#4).
2. Human beings are the proper subject of work (#5).
3. Aspects of technology (#5):
    a. positive: facilitates work;
    b. negative: can supplant or control humans.
4. Work must serve an individual's humanity (#6).

B. Materialism and Economism
1. Materialistic thought treats humans as instruments of production rather than as subjects of work (#7).
2. Workers are considered as merchandise (#7).

C. Justice and Work
1. Leo XIII's call to solidarity was a reaction against the degradation of people as subjects of work (#8).
2. Within unemployment of intellectuals, a new "proletarianization" of workers is occurring (#8).
3. Church is committed to justice for workers; it wants to be a "Church of the poor" (#8).

D. Nature of Work

1. People achieve dominion over the earth and fulfillment as human beings (#9).
2. Work and family life (#10):
   a. work makes family life possible;
   b. work makes possible the achievement of purposes of the family;
   c. it increases common good of human family.

III. Conflict between Labor and Capital

A. The Conflict

1. Conflict has changed from one between capital and labor to an ideological struggle and now to a political struggle (#11).
2. Fundamental principles (#12):
   a. priority of labor over capital;
   b. primacy of people over things.
3. Humanity has two inheritances: nature, and the resources people have developed (#12).
4. Need to develop a system that will reconcile capital and labor (#13).

B. Property

1. On ownership, Catholic social teaching differs from both Marxism (collectivism) and capitalism (#13).
2. Right of private property is subordinated to the right of common use (#14).
3. Property is acquired through work to serve labor (#14).
4. Socialization of certain means of production cannot be excluded (#14).
5. Church favors a joint-ownership of means of production (#14).

IV. Rights of Workers

Work is an obligation/duty (#16).

A. Indirect Employers

1. Indirect employers (persons, institutions, sets of principles, states, socio-economic systems) determine one or more facets of the labor relationship (#17).
2. Policies need to respect the objective rights of workers—the criterion for shaping the world economy (#17).

B. Employment

1. Suitable employment for all is needed (#18).
2. Indirect employers need to act against unemployment through (#18):

      a. unemployment benefits (springing from principle of common use of goods);

      b. a system of overall planning on economic and cultural levels;

      c. international collaboration to lessen imbalances in the standard of living.

    3. Resources must be used to create employment (#18).

C. **Workers**

    1. Just remunerations of workers is the key (#19).

    2. Wages are a practical means whereby people can have access to goods intended for the common use (#19).

    3. Church calls for (#19):

      a. wages sufficient to support a family;

      b. allowances to mothers raising a family;

      c. reevaluation of the mother's role to ensure proper love for children and fair opportunities for women.

    4. Other social benefits for workers are needed, including health care, right to leisure, pension and accident insurance, and a decent work environment (#19).

D. **Right to Form Unions**

    1. Indispensable element of social life (#20).

    2. Originated with struggles of workers (#20).

    3. Mouthpiece of the struggle for justice (#20).

    4. Constructive factor of social order (#20).

    5. Can enter political order to secure rights and the common good (#20).

    6. Strikes are legitimate but extraordinary (#20).

    7. Two cautions (#20):

      a. demands can become "class egoism";

      b. can stray from specific roles.

E. **Other**

    1. Agricultural work is the basis of healthy economies (#21).

    2. Disabled people should participate in work (#22).

    3. People have a right to leave their native countries in search of better conditions (#23).

F. **Elements of a Spirituality of Work**

    1. Humans share in the activity of their God (#25).

    2. Work imitates God's activity and gives dignity (#25).

    3. Jesus was a person of work (#26).

    4. There are many references to work in the Bible (#26).

    5. Vatican II: work allows people to fulfill their total vocation (#26).

    6. Work is sharing in the Cross and Resurrection (#27).

    7. Work is necessary for earthly progress and the development of the Kingdom (#27).

11

THE SOCIAL CONCERNS
OF THE CHURCH

*Sollicitudo Rei Socialis, Encyclical
Letter of Pope John Paul II, 1988*

Major Areas of Concern
—Authentic Development
—North/South Gap
—East/West Blocs
—Solidarity
—Option for the Poor
—Structures of Sin
—Ecological Concerns

Pope John Paul II paints a somber picture of the state of global development in *The Social Concerns of the Church*. He cites the originality of Pope Paul VI's *The Development of Peoples* and emphasizes the moral/ethical dimension of development. After surveying the difficult state of the poor countries, the Pope lays strong blame on the confrontation between the two global blocs, liberal capitalism of the West, and Marxist collectivism of the East. He refers to the obstacles hindering development as the "structures of sin" and calls for conversion toward solidarity and the option for the poor. While he does speak of the responsibilities of the poor countries, by far his strongest challenge is to the affluent world.

HISTORICAL NOTE

Twenty years after *The Development of Peoples,* Pope John Paul II celebrates that encyclical of Paul VI with a strong statement updating the Church's teaching on international development. The document reflects the severity of global economies at the end of the 1980s, with debt, unemployment, and recession seriously affecting the lives of millions not only in the developing countries but also in the more affluent countries. It echoes several of the justice-related themes addressed by the Pope in his worldwide travels.

I. **Introduction**
    1. Social doctrine seeks to lead people to respond to their vocation as responsible builders of earthly society (#1).
    2. It is marked by continuity and renewal (#3).
    3. Current encyclical celebrates twentieth anniversary of *The Development of Peoples,* and emphasizes need for fuller concept of development (#4).

II. **Originality of *The Development of Peoples***

  A. **Application of Vatican II**
    1. It responded to call of *The Church in the Modern World* (#6).
    2. It applied Council's teachings to specific problems of development and underdevelopment (#7).
  B. **Originality of Message**
    1. It emphasized ethical and cultural character of problems connected with development, and the legitimacy and necessity of Church's intervention in this field (#8).
    2. It affirmed worldwide dimension of social question, and hence the duty of solidarity between rich and poor (#9).
    3. It asserted that "development is the new name for peace," challenging the arms race and linking peace and justice (#10).

III. **Survey of Contemporary World**

  A. **Unfulfilled Hopes for Development**
    1. Twenty years ago there was widespread optimism about possibility of overcoming poverty and promoting development (#12).
    2. But in general the present situation is negative (#13):

  a. innumerable multitudes suffer intolerable burden of poverty;
  b. many millions have lost hope, seeing their situation worsened.
B. **Widened Gap between North and South**
  1. Developing countries are falling behind developed in terms of production and distribution of basics (#14).
  2. Unity of world is compromised, with division into First, Second, Third, Fourth Worlds (#14).
  3. Cultural underdevelopment shown in: illiteracy, lack of participation, exploitation, religious oppression, racial discrimination, etc. (#15).
  4. Right of economic initiative, for service of the common good, is often suppressed, frustrating people's creativity (#15).
  5. Totalitarianism makes people "objects" (#15).
  6. Other forms of poverty exist, e.g., denial of human rights such as right to religious freedom (#15).
  7. Causes of worsened situation include (#16):
    a. omissions on part of developing countries;
    b. lack of response by affluent world;
    c. mechanisms (economic, political, social) manipulated to benefit some at the expense of others.
  8. Interdependence separated from ethical requirements is disastrous for both rich and poor countries (#17).
C. **Specific Signs of Underdevelopment**
  1. Housing crisis, experienced universally, is due largely to increasing urbanization (#17).
  2. Unemployment and underemployment grow, raising serious questions about the type of development pursued (#18).
  3. Global debt, forcing debtor nations to export capital, is aggravating underdevelopment (#19).
D. **Political Reasons for Underdevelopment**
  1. Existence of two opposing blocs, East and West, has considerable impact on development of people (#20).
  2. Political opposition rests on deeper ideological opposition (#20):
    a. liberal capitalism of the West;
    b. Marxist collectivism of the East.
  3. Military opposition results, with tensions of "cold war," "wars by proxy" (#21).
  4. Church's social doctrine is critical toward both liberal capitalism and Marxist collectivism (#21).
  5. Recently independent countries become involved in, sometimes overwhelmed by, ideological conflict, as two blocs tend toward imperialism and neo-colonialism (#'s 21–22).
  6. Exaggerated concern for security blocks cooperation (#22).

       a. Competition between two blocs prevents leadership and solidarity (#23).

       b. West abandons self to growing and selfish isolation (#23).

       c. East ignores duty to alleviate human misery (#23).

   7. Arms trade flourishes, refugees are created, and terrorism increases (#24).

   8. Demographic problem is often met without respect for persons (#25).

E. Positive Aspects of Contemporary World

   1. Awareness grows of dignity and human rights, as expressed in UN's *Declaration of Human Rights* (#26).

   2. Conviction increases regarding radical interdependence and solidarity (#26).

   3. Peace is seen as indivisible; it is for all, and demands justice (#26).

   4. Ecological concern grows, with recognition of limited resources and need to respect nature (#26).

   5. Generous persons sacrifice for peace, and international organizations contribute to more effective action (#26).

   6. Some Third World countries have reached food self-sufficiency (#26).

IV. Authentic Human Development

A. Challenges to Development

   1. Development is not straightforward "progress" in Enlightenment sense (#27).

   2. After world wars and with atomic peril, "naive mechanistic optimism" has been replaced by "well-founded anxiety" (#27).

   3. Narrow economic emphasis is questioned (#28).

   4. Side-by-side with miseries of underdevelopment is inadmissible superdevelopment which involves consumerism and waste (#28).

   5. "Having" does not contribute to human perfection unless it contributes to maturing and enriching of "being" (#28).

   6. One of the greatest injustices in contemporary world: "poor distribution of the goods and services originally intended for all" (#28).

   7. "Having" can detract from "being" if one disregards the quality and ordered hierarchy of the goods one has (#28).

B. Development and Human Nature

1. True development calls for recognition of spiritual, transcendent nature of human beings (#29).
2. Biblical story shows humans developing (#30):
   a. having dominion over creation but obedient to Creator;
   b. falling into sin but responding to divine call.
3. Faith in Christ reveals plan for reconciliation of all to him (#31).
4. Church therefore has pastoral duty to concern itself with problems of development (#31).
5. Early teachers of Church had optimistic vision of history and work (#31).
6. Church cannot ignore needs of the poor in favor of "superfluous church ornaments and costly furnishings for divine worship" (#31).

C. Cooperation for Development

1. This task is not individualistic; there is an obligation to collaborate with all others in this field (#32).
2. People and nations have a right to their own development (#32).
3. Moral character of development requires recognition of rights (#33):
   a. at internal level, respecting life, family, employment, political community, religion;
   b. at international level, respecting peoples, culture, equality of all;
   c. within framework of solidarity and freedom.

D. Respect for Natural World

1. There is growing awareness of the "cosmos"—the natural order of all beings, living and inanimate (#34).
2. Natural resources are limited and cannot be used with absolute dominion (#34).
3. Pollution of the environment threatens the health of all (#34).

V. Theological Reading of Modern Problems

A. Situation of Sin

1. In years since *The Development of Peoples,* "there has been no development—or very little, irregular, or even contradictory development" (#35).
2. Main obstacle to development is not political but moral (#35).

3. World divided into blocs, sustained by ideologies, and dominated by imperialism is a world "subject to structures of sin" (#36).
4. Individual actions against neighbor introduce into world influences and obstacles that go beyond individuals, interfering with the development of peoples (#36).
5. Two typical structures of sin are (#37):
    a. all-consuming desire for profit;
    b. thirst for power, imposing one's will on others.

B. **Path of Conversion**
1. Profound attitudes which define relationships with self, neighbor, and nature must be changed (#38).
2. "Conversion" is needed, toward interdependency, solidarity, commitment to common good (#38).
3. Solidarity requires (#39):
    a. on part of influential, a responsibility and willingness to share;
    b. on part of weaker, an active claiming of rights.
4. Church has evangelical duty to stand by the poor (#39).
5. Solidarity helps us see the "other" as "neighbor," "helper," and is the path to peace and development (#39).
6. As Christian virtue, solidarity is rooted in vision of human beings in relationship to Trinity (#40).

VI. Some Particular Guidelines

A. **Church's Social Doctrine**
1. Church offers not technical solutions but "set of principles for reflection, criteria for judgment, and directives for action" (#41).
2. It is not a "third way" between liberal capitalism and Marxist collectivism (#42):
    a. not an ideology but a theological interpretation;
    b. a condemnation/proclamation as part of prophetic role.
3. Today especially it must be open to international outlook (#42).

B. **Option for the Poor**
1. Whole tradition of Church bears witness to "love of preference for the poor," a special form of primacy in exercise of Christian charity (#42).
2. This affects individual action and applies equally to social responsibilities (#42).

3. Growing numbers of poor, in desperate situations, must be a priority in all development plans (#42).
4. The goods of the world are originally meant for all, and hence private property has a "social mortgage" (#42).
5. Special form of poverty includes being deprived of rights, particularly right to religious freedom and right to freedom of economic initiative (#42).

C. Imbalance of International System

1. International trade system discriminates against developing countries, and international division of labor exploits workers for profit (#43).
2. World monetary and financial system compounds poorer countries' problems of balance of payments and debt (#43).
3. Technology transfer is unfair to poorer countries (#43).
4. International organizations need reform, without being manipulated by political rivalries (#43).

D. Responsibilities of Developing Countries

1. Developing countries must take up their own responsibilities (#44).
2. They should promote self-affirmation of their own citizens through programs of literacy and basic education (#44).
3. They need to set priorities (#44):
   a. food production;
   b. reform of political structures;
   c. promotion of human rights.
4. Solidarity among developing countries will call for greater cooperation and establishment of effective regional organizations (#45).

VII. Conclusion

A. True Liberation

1. There is an intimate connection between liberation and development, overcoming obstacles to a "more human life" (#46).
2. Church affirms possibility of overcoming the obstacles, with confidence in the goodness of humans (#47).

B. Urgent Appeal

1. Everyone must be convinced of seriousness of moment and of responsibility to take steps "inspired by solidarity and love of preference for the poor" (#47).
2. As agents of peace and justice, laity have preeminent role in animating temporal realities with Christian commitment (#47).

3. Special cooperation urged with other Christians, with Jews, and with followers of world's great religions (#47).
4. The fact that the Kingdom of God is not identified with any temporal achievement cannot excuse us from lack of concern for concrete situations of today (#48).
5. Eucharist is special call to commitment to development and peace (#48).
6. In Marian Year, we ask Mary's intercession in this difficult moment of the modern world (#49).

12

THE CHURCH AND RACISM

Statement of the Pontifical Justice and Peace Commission, 1988

Major Areas of Concern
—Racism
—Anti-Semitism
—Human Dignity
—Solidarity
—Conscience Formation

The document notes that racism, as in the past, continues to trouble the world today. It examines different manifestations of racism and firmly restates the traditional Catholic principles of human dignity and solidarity. The document gives the Church the role of changing hearts and offering a place for reconciliation in the hope that structural change may follow.

HISTORICAL NOTE

This statement, released February 10, 1989, is the first Vatican document to deal exclusively with racism. It closely followed Pope John Paul II's September 1988 visit to Southern Africa, and reflected his concern for the persistence of apartheid. The approaching quincentenary of Columbus' voyage to America was also renewing interest in the relation between evangelization and colonization.

Introduction

1. Racial prejudice continues to trouble the world (#1).
2. The Holy See "has the duty to denounce deplorable situations prophetically" (#1).

I. Racist Behavior throughout History

1. Racism has long been a part of human history (#2).
2. With colonization of the Americas, theologians and missionaries defended the indigenous people (#3).
3. Because of the patronage system, the Church was not always able to make the necessary pastoral decisions for the indigenous people (#3).
4. The Apostolic See frequently insisted on a distinction between evangelization and imperialism (#5).
5. The memory of crimes such as Nazi racism should never be erased (#7).

II. Forms of Racism Today

1. Racism is manifested in exclusion and aggression (#8).
2. Institutional racism (apartheid in South Africa) is "unacceptable." Dialogue is needed to overcome prejudice and create peaceful evolution (#9).
3. Aboriginal peoples have been marginalized or victimized by genocide. They should be integrated into society on the basis of their free choice (#10).
4. Religious or ethnic criteria for civil or religious rights should be abolished (#11).
5. Ethnocentric attitudes can cause grave problems and should be changed (#12).
6. Social racism can create new forms of racism in the Third World (#13).
7. Spontaneous racism, especially toward foreigners, is "reprehensible" (#14).
8. Anti-Semitism is the most tragic form of racism (#15).
9. With artificial procreation and the possibility of genetic manipulation, new forms of racism may emerge (#16).

III. The Dignity of Every Race and the Unity of Humankind

1. The Christian doctrine of the human person, enlightened by biblical revelation, holds that all people are created in God's

image and have the same nature, calling, and divine destiny (#17).

2. The principle of equal dignity finds substantial support in the sciences, philosophy, ethics, and other religions (#18).
3. Faith in God should absolutely negate racist ideology (#19).
4. Revelation insists on the unity of the human family (#20).
5. Christ made all the marginalized—Samaritans, pagans, the sick, sinners, prostitutes—beneficiaries of salvation (#21).
6. The Church must realize, first within herself, the unity of humankind (#22).
7. Christian teaching calls for respect for differences, fraternity, and solidarity (#23).

IV. The Contributions of Christians

1. Racism begins in the heart and must be purified (#24).
2. The Bible should never be used to justify racism (#25).
3. Victims of racism must be defended (#26).
4. The Church evangelically tries to prepare a change in mentality that enables structural change (#27).
5. Schools are important in forming non-racist consciences (#28).
6. Laws must be equal for all citizens and guarantee basic human rights for non-citizens (#29).
7. Internationally, juridical instruments to combat racism must be fostered and followed (#30).
8. The Christian communities in the U.S. and South Africa both have opposed racism (#31).
9. Racism can affect international peace (#32).

Conclusion

1. The effort to overcome racism has become broadly anchored in the human conscience (#33).
2. All discrimination must be opposed (#33).
3. The Church wants to change hearts and offer a place for reconciliation (#33).

13

THE MISSIONARY ACTIVITY OF THE CHURCH

Redemptoris Missio, Encyclical Letter of Pope John Paul II, 1990

Major Areas of Concern
—Liberation
—Base Communities
—Local Churches
—Inculturation
—Poverty

The encyclical begins by affirming that the Church's mission is far from completion. It goes on to deal with many facets of this mission especially insofar as it applies to non-Christian places. The letter treats such topics as liberation and inculturation. Pope John Paul II supports economic and political liberation but cautions that one finds true liberation only in Christ. He confirms the importance of an inculturation that maintains communion with the universal church. In this encyclical, the Pope emphasizes the role of local communities and churches in missionary activity.

HISTORICAL NOTE

This encyclical, released January 22, 1991, commemorates the twenty-fifth anniversary of Vatican II's decree *Ad Gentes*. The encyclical argues

against what the Pope perceives as a tendency on the part of some missionaries to neglect the explicitly Christian dimensions of missionary activity in
favor simply of economic liberation or humanistic activity. The letter's affirmation of interreligious dialogue is most likely an attempt to bolster the
church's position in the Muslim regions of Africa.

Introduction

1. The mission of the Church is far from completion (#1).
2. The missionary fruit of Vatican II includes:
   a. an increase in local churches with their own bishops;
   b. a more evident presence of Christian communities in the life
      of nations;
   c. increased commitment and involvement of laity (#2).
3. Internal and external difficulties have weakened the Church's
   missionary activity to non-Christians (#2).
4. Missionary evangelization is the primary service the Church
   can render to the world (#2).

I. Jesus Christ, the Only Savior

1. Christ is the one savior of all (#5).
2. The urgency of missionary activity flows from the new life of
   Jesus (#7).
3. Proclaiming and witnessing to Christ, when respectful of consciences, does not violate human freedom (#8).
4. True liberation consists in opening oneself to the love of Christ
   (#11).
5. A temptation today is to reduce Christianity to merely human
   wisdom (#11).

II. The Kingdom of God

1. The proclamation of the Kingdom—already at work in our
   midst—is the mission of Jesus (#13).
2. The Kingdom is meant for all humankind (#14).
3. Building the Kingdom means working for liberation from all
   evil (#15).
4. The Kingdom is not merely economic and political liberation;
   it has Christocentric and transcendental dimensions too
   (#17).
5. The Church is at the service of the Kingdom (#20).

III. The Holy Spirit

1. The Holy Spirit is the principal agent of the Church's mission (#21).
2. The gospels point to a pluralism, reflecting different experiences of communities, within the Church's fundamental unity (#23).
3. The Spirit works in the Church and also in the heart of every person (#28).
4. The Church respects the action of the Spirit in persons of other religions (#29).
5. Responsibility for the discernment of the presence of the Spirit lies with the Church (#29).

IV. The Horizons of Mission "Ad Gentes"

1. The Church's mission "ad gentes" is most properly addressed to areas where the Gospel is not known or Christian communities are not sufficiently mature (#34).
2. Indifferentism to mission is based on incorrect theological perspectives and religious relativism (#36).
3. The Church's mission "ad gentes" should be primarily directed towards Asia (#37).
4. In situations of widespread poverty, the proclamation of Christ must be the means for restoring human dignity (#37).
5. In the midst of consumerism and materialism people are searching for a meaning which the Church can offer (#38).
6. Today the majority of believers and particular churches are no longer found in Europe (#40).

V. The Paths of Mission

1. Witness by missionaries, families, and communities is most important (#43).
2. The Church is called to witness by taking prophetic stands in face of corruption of political or economic power (#43).
3. The proclamation of the Word aims at a conversion to a faith which is total and radical (#46).
4. The objective of the mission "ad gentes" is to form Christian communities and local churches (#48).
5. Ecumenical activity can aid missionary activity (#50).
6. Base communities, founded on Christ, are a sign of vitality in the Church (#51).
7. Through inculturation, the Church becomes more intelligible and more effective (#52).

8. Inculturation must be guided by:
   a. compatibility with the Gospel;
   b. communion with the universal Church (#54).
9. Interreligious dialogue is a path toward the kingdom (#57).
10. The Church, through the Gospel, offers a force for liberation that springs from conversion (#59).
11. The Church is called to be on the side of the poor and oppressed (#60).

VI. Leaders and Workers in Mission

1. Young churches should share in the universal missionary work of the Church as soon as possible (#62).
2. The college of bishops and the pope are primarily responsible for missionary activity (#63).
3. A missionary vocation is special and should be fostered (#65).
4. Laity—individuals, families, and communities—play an important role in missionary activity (#71).

VII. Cooperation in Mission

1. Cooperation is expressed "above all" in promoting missionary vocations (#79).
2. Sharing in the sacrifice of missionaries necessitates a reassessment in the way of living (#81).
3. Tourists should respect the nations they visit (#82).
4. Missionary activity involves liberation, development, defense of human rights, and, most of all, promoting faith (#83).
5. There is a new consensus among peoples about values:
   a. rejection of violence and war;
   b. respect for human persons and rights;
   c. desire for freedom, justice, and brotherhood;
   d. surmounting of some racism and nationalism;
   e. affirmation of the dignity and role of women (#86).

VIII. Missionary Spirituality

1. Characteristics of missionary spirituality include:
   a. docility to the Holy Spirit (#87);
   b. intimate communion with Christ (#88);
   c. apostolic charity and zeal for souls (#89);
   d. profound love for the Church (#89);
   e. the cultivation of holiness (#90).
2. Young churches will be a leaven of missionary spirit for the older churches (#91).

14

ONE HUNDRED YEARS

Centesimus Annus, Encyclical Letter of Pope John Paul II, 1991

Major Areas of Concern
—Human Dignity
—Human Rights
—Justice
—Development
—Peace
—Economic Systems

One Hundred Years (Centesimus Annus) begins with a restatement and a current application of the major principles of *On the Condition of Labor (Rerum Novarum)*. Pope John Paul II then addresses the relationship of the Church's social teaching to major trends and events in the past one hundred years with a special emphasis on the events in Eastern Europe in 1989. He misses no opportunity to affirm human dignity and human rights. The encyclical notes the fall of "Real Socialism," but cautions against thinking that this fall signifies a victory for capitalism.

HISTORICAL NOTE

Centesimus Annus was promulgated in May 1991, after the collapse of socialism in most of Eastern Europe and the conclusion of the Persian Gulf War, but before the collapse of the Communist Party in the Soviet Union.

The encyclical, the ninth of John Paul II's pontificate, commemorates the one hundredth anniversary of *Rerum Novarum*.

Introduction

1. *Rerum Novarum* is of "great importance" for the Church; the "vital energies" it unleashed continue to increase (#1).
2. *Rerum Novarum* can be used to help look back at fundamental principles, "look around" at new events, and look to the future (#3).
3. An analysis of history and current events is essential to the Church's mission of evangelization (#3).

I. Characteristics of Rerum Novarum

1. *Rerum Novarum* attempted to address a new conception of society, the state, and authority, especially as manifested in the conflict between capital and labor (#'s 4–5).
2. Leo XIII gave the Church a paradigm and a corpus to analyze, judge, and indicate directions for social realities (#5).
3. To teach and spread her social doctrine is an essential part of the Church's evangelizing mission (#5).
4. There can be no genuine solution to the "social question" apart from the Gospel (#5).
5. *Rerum Novarum* strongly affirms the dignity of work, the right to private property and the complementary principle of "the universal destination of the earth's goods," as well as the rights to private associations, limited working hours, legitimate rest, a family wage, and to discharge freely religious duties (#'s 6–9).
6. *Rerum Novarum*'s criticism of socialism and liberalism is still relevant today, as is the principle that the poor and defenseless have a claim to special consideration—what we now call the principle of solidarity (#10).
7. *Rerum Novarum*'s emphasis on the rights of the poor and the defenseless gives testimony to the continuity of the option for the poor (#11).
8. The guiding light of *Rerum Novarum* is its view of human dignity (#11).

II. Toward the "New Things" of Today

1. In responding to the harsh condition of the working class, socialism suppressed private property and fundamentally mis-

understood the human person as simply an element in society (#'s 12–13).

2. According to the Christian vision of the person, his/her social nature is realized in various intermediary groups, always with a view to the common good. The error of socialism springs from atheism and results in a distortion of law and human freedom (#13).

3. Atheism and contempt for the human person cause class struggle and militarism (#14).

4. The State, respectful of the principles of subsidiarity and solidarity, has a positive role to play in determining the juridical framework of economic affairs. The State and the society are both responsible for protecting workers from unemployment, providing adequate wages, training, and humane working hours (#15).

5. The role of the workers' movement in economic reform has been an important one (#16).

6. *Rerum Novarum* opposed ideologies of hatred and showed how violence could be overcome by justice (#17).

7. Since 1945, in Europe, there has been a situation of non-war but not genuine peace:
   a. many people lost the ability to control their own destiny;
   b. an "insane" arms race swallowed up vital resources;
   c. violent extremist groups found ready support;
   d. the atomic threat oppressed the world (#18).

8. After World War II, there were some positive efforts to rebuild democratic societies inspired by social justice. They generally preserved free market mechanisms while subjecting them to public control, "which upholds the principle of the common destination of material goods." Systems of national security states and consumer societies were also set up to oppose Marxism (#19).

9. After World War II, decolonization occurred. Genuine independence of developing nations is impeded by foreign economic and political control and the lack of a competent professional class (#20).

10. Since 1945, the awareness of human rights—with the United Nations as a focal point—has grown (#21).

11. It is necessary now to remedy the grave imbalances between geographical areas; they have shifted the center of the social question from the national to the international level (#21).

12. The UN has not yet succeeded in establishing a continuously favorable development aid policy or an effective system of conflict resolution as an alternative to war (#21).

III. The Year 1989

1. In 1989:
   a. in Eastern Europe, oppressive regimes fell;
   b. some Third World countries began a transition to more just and participatory structures (#22).
2. The Church's commitment to defend and promote human rights was an important contribution to the events of 1989 (#22).
3. Factors that contributed to the fall of oppressive regimes:
   a. violation of workers' rights (#23);
   b. inefficiency of the economic system (#24);
   c. spiritual void brought about by atheism (#24).
4. Non-violent, peaceful protest accomplished almost all of the changes in Eastern Europe (#23).
5. The events of 1989 would be unthinkable without prayer and trust in God. We must remember that no political society will be perfect, no society should be confused with the Reign of God (#25).
6. The events of 1989 illustrate opportunities for human freedom to cooperate with the plan of God who acts in history (#26).
7. In some countries, the events of 1989 resulted from an encounter between the Church and the workers' movement (#26).
8. The events of 1989 illustrated that the Church's social doctrine of (as well as concrete commitment to) integral human liberation does not necessitate an "impossible" compromise between Christianity and Marxism (#26).
9. International structures that can help rebuild, economically and morally, the countries that have abandoned communism are needed (#27).
10. Marxism's fall has highlighted human interdependence (#27).
11. Peace and prosperity are goods that belong to the whole human race (#27).
12. Aid for Eastern Europe, without a slackening of aid for the Third World, is "a debt in justice." Plentiful resources can be made available through disarmament, developing reliable procedures for resolving conflicts, and taking appropriate measures against the arms trade (#28).
13. There must be a change in priorities and values on which economic and political choices are made (#28).
14. The advancement of the poor is an opportunity for the moral, cultural and economic growth of all humanity (#28).
15. Development must be seen in fully human, and not merely economic, terms (#29).

IV. Private Property and the Universality of Material Goods

1. Catholic social teaching affirms a right to private property that is limited by the common purpose of goods (#30).
2. The foundation of the common purpose of all goods or "the universal destination of the earth's goods" is the original source of all good things in the gift of God's creation for all. Human work on this creation is the foundation of private property. More and more, human work is work with and for others (#31).
3. The possession of know-how, technology, and skill is surpassing land as the decisive factor of production (#32).
4. The majority of people today do not have the means or the possibility of acquiring the basic knowledge to enter the world of technology and intercommunication. They are thus exploited or marginalized (#33).
5. The human inadequacies of capitalism are far from disappearing (#33).
6. Many human needs are not satisfied by the market. "It is a strict duty of justice and truth not to allow fundamental human needs to remain unsatisfied, and not to allow those burdened by such needs to perish" (#34).
7. It is also a requirement of human dignity to help needy people acquire expertise and develop the skill to enter the modern economy. There must be a family wage, social insurance for old age and unemployment, and good working conditions (#34).
8. The State needs to control the market to guarantee that the basic needs of society are satisfied (#35).
9. A business firm is a community of persons, endeavoring to meet their basic needs, who form a group at the service of society (#35).
10. Human and moral factors are just as important as profit to the life of a business (#35).
11. The defeat of "Real Socialism" does not leave capitalism as the only model of economic organization (#35).
12. Stronger nations must offer weaker nations the opportunity to take their place in the international order (#35).
13. The foreign debt of poorer countries needs to be handled in a way that respects the rights of people to subsistence and progress (#35).
14. Consumerism has created attitudes and lifestyles which damage the physical and spiritual health of human beings (#36).
15. It is necessary to create lifestyles which emphasize being rather than having, in which the quest for truth, beauty, goodness, and

the common good determine consumer choices, savings and investment decisions (#36).

16. Producers of products, the mass media, and public authorities have a special role to play in fostering a sense of general responsibility (#36).

17. The ecological questions reveal human greed and irresponsibility in the face of obligations to future generations (#37).

18. There must also be serious effort to protect the moral conditions for authentic "human ecology," to address the problems of urbanization through a "social ecology" of work, and to destroy and replace social structures of sin, which impede full human realization (#38).

19. The family, founded on marriage, is the sanctuary of life (#39).

20. There are goods which are not and cannot be mere commodities that are bought and sold. The State must defend and preserve such common goods as the natural and human environments, which are essential frameworks for the legitimate pursuit of personal goals (#40).

21. True human alienation happens in consumerism, conditions of work that are not concerned about the personal development of the worker, and social relationships marked by competition, estrangement and the use of people as means to one's ends. Overcoming it requires the free gift of self to others in community (#41).

22. Should capitalism be the goal for countries? If "capitalism" means a system that recognizes the positive role of business, the market, private property endowed with a sense of responsibility for the means of production, and free human creativity, the answer is "Yes." If "capitalism" means a system in which economic freedom is not circumscribed within a strong juridical framework which directs it in service to the common good and of larger ethical and religious values, the answer is "No" (#42).

23. The collapse of the communist system risks the rise of a radical capitalist ideology which entrusts everything to the free development of market forces (#42).

24. The Church's social teaching should serve as an orientation, rather than as a model, toward solving these problems.
    a. It recognizes the positive value of market and of enterprise as long as they are oriented to the common good.
    b. It acknowledges the need for a broad, organized labor movement directed toward the liberation and promotion of the whole person in service of family and community.
    c. It judges ownership of the means of production as just and legitimate when it serves useful work, but as unjust and ille-

gitimate when it impedes, exploits or eliminates work or breaks worker solidarity in pursuit of profit "which is not the result of overall expansion of work and the wealth of society" (#43).

V. State and Culture

1. Modern totalitarianism denies objective truth and relies on the force of power. It is rooted in a denial of the transcendental dignity of the human person (#44).

2. In defending its own freedom against totalitarianism's rejection of objective criteria for good and evil and absorption of communities into itself, the Church defends the dignity of the human person (#45).

3. The Church values any democratic system that ensures its citizens' ability to participate in it and hold those in power accountable (#46).

4. Democratic systems need to solidify their foundations by explicitly recognizing certain rights, especially the rights to life, to family, to education, to work, to establish a family and to religious freedom (#47).

5. If these rights are not fully respected and decisions are made on the basis of electoral or financial power rather than criteria of justice and morality, political participation and civic spirit will decline. Particular interests will not be situated within the common good, which involves assessing and integrating those interests on the basis of a balanced hierarchy of values grounded in a correct understanding of the dignity and rights of persons (#47).

6. Principal tasks of the State include:
   a. guaranteeing economic security,
   b. overseeing and directing the exercise of human rights in the economy,
   c. creating conditions which will ensure job opportunities,
   d. regulating monopolies,
   e. substituting for or protecting weak systems just getting under way,
   f. responding to social needs according to the principle of subsidiarity (#48).

7. The Church—through charity, solidarity, and volunteer work—has always been among the needy. It is committed to the truth that life in society has community as its final purpose, not the market or the state (#49).

8. A culture achieves its character through the search for truth. When it becomes inward looking and rejects any exchange or

debate about human truth, it becomes sterile and decadent (#50).

9. The Church's contribution to culture is to form human hearts for peace and justice, reminding them that they are progressively responsible for the whole human community (#51).

10. A culture of peace needs to promote development and provide the poor with realistic opportunities. This requires interventions on the international as well as the national level (#52).

11. This task may necessitate changes in lifestyle that reduce the waste of resources (#52).

12. New material and spiritual resources are required which come from the work and culture of poor and marginalized peoples (#52).

VI. Humans as the Way of the Church

1. The Church's purpose is the care and responsibility not only for humankind, but also for each individual (#53).

2. The Church's social teaching is an instrument of evangelization for salvation (#54).

3. The Church receives the "meaning of humankind" from Divine Revelation (#55).

4. The Western countries run the risk of seeing the collapse of "Real Socialism" as a victory for their own systems and may fail to make necessary changes in those systems (#56).

5. The social basis of the Gospel must function as a basis and motivation for action because witnessing for justice and peace is more credible than logical arguments (#57).

6. The option for the poor is not limited to material poverty but encompasses cultural and spiritual poverty as well (#57).

7. Love is made concrete in the promotion of justice which requires changes in lifestyles, models of production and consumption, and structures of power (#58).

8. Globalization of the economy ought to be accompanied by effecting international agencies to oversee and direct the economy to the common good. This requires increased coordination among the more powerful nations and consideration of the most needy (#58).

9. Grace is needed for the demands of justice to be met (#59).

10. The Church's social teaching enters into dialogue with the other disciplines concerned with humankind (#59).

11. People who profess no religious beliefs as well as members of the Christian churches and all great world religions will have a

preeminent role in preserving peace and building a truly human society (#60).

12. Society should be free of oppression and built on a spirit of cooperation and solidarity. The Church will denounce poverty and injustice although this call will not find favor with all (#61).

15

The Catechism of the Catholic Church, 1992

Major Areas of Concern
—Common Good
—Human Dignity
—Solidarity
—Love of the Poor
—Participation
—Peace

The Catechism includes a succinct and authoritative compilation of the principles and major themes of Catholic social teaching. Pope John Paul II calls it an "authentic reference text" in the universal Church for the teaching of Catholic doctrine. While the Catechism delineates the Church's social teachings extensively in three sections in its third part (of four), the major principles and themes are woven throughout the document's 2,865 paragraphs. The Catechism makes it clear that social teachings are an integral part of—and not an appendix to—the Catholic faith. In his introduction to the document, Pope John Paul II states the Catechism "is meant to encourage and assist in the writing of new local catechisms, which take into account various situations and cultures, while carefully preserving the unity of faith and fidelity to Catholic doctrine." The Catechism cites extensively previous documents in the Church's social tradition, in particular, *The Church in the Modern World (Gaudium et Spes)* and *One Hundred Years (Centesimus Annus)*.

HISTORICAL NOTE

The Catechism was promulgated in 1992 to coincide with the thirtieth anniversary of the opening of the Second Vatican Council. Its English translation was published in 1994. The Catechism represents the work over a six-year period of a commission of twelve prelates, chaired by Cardinal Joseph Ratzinger. It is the first new Catechism in the life of the universal Church since the Catechism of St. Pius V in 1566.

Note: This outline does not attempt to summarize the entire Catechism, only the areas treating Catholic social teaching. The first three sections in the outline correspond to the three chapters in Part Three of the Catechism in which this treatment is most extensive. The final section brings together material from various places in the document.

I. The Human Community

A. The Person and Society

1. All persons are called to God and to union with all other people. Love of God and neighbor are inseparable (#1878).
2. Humans are social by nature and develop only in society. Each person inherits talents and skills from the society and owes the society loyalty. At the same time, each person is the principle, subject and end of society (#'s 1879–1881).
3. National and international voluntary institutions should promote the widest participation in a society. This promotes initiative and responsibility while protecting human rights (#1882).
4. The principle of subsidiarity protects personal freedom and initiative, diffuses power, and harmonizes individual and social relationships, even to the establishment of true international order (#'s 1883–1885).
5. Personal conversion is essential to social change and requires changing unjust social institutions and living conditions that promote sin (#1888).
6. Charity respects the rights of all and demands justice (#1889).

B. Participation in Social Life

1. Society requires authority to promote and protect the good of all and the unity of the state. Thus grounded in human nature, authority is ultimately from God and deserves due respect (#'s 1897–1900).
2. Diverse forms of authority are legitimate only when they seek the common good using morally legitimate means. Each power should be balanced by other powers in a rule of law (#'s 1901–1904).

3. The common good is the sum of those social conditions that allow all people to develop. It demands respect for the fundamental rights and freedoms essential to persons' development, the social well-being and development of the group (making basic necessities such as food, clothing, health, work, education, culture, and information available to all), and peace in a stable, secure and just order (#'s 1906–1909).

4. The state must defend and promote the common good (#1910).

5. Growing global interdependence implies a universal common good, which requires a global authority to defend and promote it (#1911).

6. The common good serves the progress of persons, always subordinating things to persons (#1912).

7. All must participate in promoting the common good by assuming responsibility for personal and family needs and being active in public life (#'s 1913–1915).

8. This ethical obligation requires constant conversion to promote just institutions that improve the conditions of life for all (#1916).

9. Those with authority must inspire people with confidence, reasons for living, and a spirit of service (#1917).

C. **Social Justice**

1. Social justice exists when society provides the conditions necessary for individuals and organizations to pursue their goals. It is grounded in human dignity and the rights that flow from that dignity. Society does not give these rights; it must recognize them if it is to have legitimacy and moral authority. The role of the Church is to remind people of all human rights and to distinguish them from false claims (#'s 1928–1930).

2. Respect for persons means loving them as we love ourselves. This is especially important toward the disadvantaged, those who are different from us, and all our enemies (#'s 1931–1933).

3. All are created in God's image and redeemed by Christ. All have equal dignity, and discrimination on the basis of sex, race, color, social conditions, language or religion is against God's plan (#'s 1934–1935).

4. People's gifts and talents differ so that they need one another and are drawn to share and care for each other. Excessive economic and social disparities are a scandal and a contradiction of God's plan (#'s 1936–1938).

5. Solidarity is a form of social friendship and is an essential demand of Christian community. It requires the distribution of

material and spiritual goods, just pay for work, and negotiation of conflicts. World peace requires solidarity among those in poverty, among workers, between rich and poor, between employers and employees, and between nations and peoples (#'s 1939–1942).

II. Loving One's Neighbor

A. Ownership of Goods

1. The goods of creation were intended for everyone; that is the primordial reality. Private property is legitimate to meet basic needs and protect freedom and dignity, but it does not override the universal purpose of all goods (#'s 2401–2403).
2. Everything people own is also meant to serve the common good and should be used "in ways that will benefit the greatest number" (#2405).
3. Government can and must regulate property ownership to serve the common good (#2406).

B. Respect for Persons, Their Goods, and the Integrity of Creation

1. Respect for human dignity demands that people not become too attached to goods (temperance), honor each other's rights and needs (justice), and be in solidarity with all (#2407).
2. Stealing others' property is forbidden unless there is an obvious and urgent necessity to meet basic needs (#2408).
3. Unjustly keeping others' property, whether borrowed or found, paying unjust wages, overcharging, financial speculation, corruption, tax evasion, forgery, waste and vandalism are all forbidden (#2409).
4. Morally just promises and contracts must be kept under the virtue of commutative justice. Commutative justice also requires protecting property rights, paying debts, and making restitution for stolen goods (#'s 2410–2412).
5. Slavery and trafficking in persons are also forbidden (#2414).
6. Since creation is for the well-being of all, people's relationship with animals, plants and all of creation must be one of stewardship guided by respectful care for them and moral concern for the common good of current and future generations. Money needed to help human beings in misery should not be spent on animals (#'s 2415–2418).

C. The Social Doctrine of the Church

1. The Church interprets the Gospel to explain the demands of justice and peace in order to protect fundamental rights and save souls (#'s 2419–2420).
2. The Church's social teaching develops to address changing structures of production, society, authority, labor and owner-

ship. Its principles, criteria and guidelines for action will be more widely accepted if the faithful live them (#'s 2421–2423).

3. The Church rejects the totalitarianism and atheism of communism as well as its subordination of people's basic rights to collectivism. It rejects the individualism of capitalism, its idolatry of profit, and the primacy of the laws of the market over workers. Markets and economic activities must be regulated in accord with just values and for the common good (#'s 2424–2425).

D. **Economic Activity and Social Justice**

1. Economic life is to serve individuals and the entire human community (#2426).

2. Human work is the continuation of God's creation, a duty, a means of personal development, redemption, and sanctification. The value of the work comes from the person doing it, who should be able to provide for personal and family needs through it (#'s 2427–2428).

3. Everyone has the right to take economic initiatives in accord with legitimate regulation to serve the common good. Conflicts of interest should be resolved through negotiation (#'s 2429–2430).

4. The responsibility of the state is to guarantee individual freedom, private property, a stable currency, efficient public services, and the protection of human rights (#2431).

5. Business leaders are responsible for the economic and ecological effects of their operations, for the good of persons and communities as well as profits (#2432).

6. Society should guarantee access to employment and the professions without unjust discrimination and should help people find work (#2433).

7. A just wage must meet the material, social, cultural and spiritual needs of the person and the family, taking account of the person's role, contribution, the state of the business, and the common good (#2434).

8. Recourse to a strike is morally legitimate when it is unavoidable, proportionate, related to working conditions, non-violent, and in accord with the common good (#2435).

E. **Justice and Solidarity among Nations**

1. There is a serious gap between wealthy and poor nations that must be overcome in a spirit of solidarity, especially when it is necessary to replace unjust financial systems, commercial relations, and arms trading with common efforts to achieve more authentic moral, cultural and economic development (#'s 2437–2438).

2. Rich nations have a grave moral responsibility in solidarity,

charity, and often in justice to help nations unable to or prevented from guaranteeing their own development (#2439).

3. Direct aid is necessary as disaster relief, but it is also necessary to reform international economic and financial institutions to promote more just international relationships and support growth and liberation in poor nations, especially in agriculture (#2440).

4. Full human development includes an increased sense of God, increased self-awareness, the development of more material goods at the service of people and their freedom, the reduction of dire poverty and economic exploitation, growing respect for cultural identities, and openness to the transcendent (#2441).

5. It is the role of the laity to establish this gospel vision in the organization of society (#2442).

F. Love for the Poor

1. Love for the poor is the sign of a follower of Christ. It demands that we share with them what we have, for it is theirs as well in justice (#'s 2443–2446).

2. The corporal and spiritual "works of mercy" are ways to realize the Church's preferential love for those oppressed by poverty and living in misery (#'s 2447–2448).

3. Jesus built on the legal measures of care for the poor in the Old Testament by proclaiming his presence in the poor (#2449).

III. Safeguarding Peace

A. Legitimate Defense

1. Human life is sacred because it is from and for God. Defending one's life is therefore legitimate, though one should not intend to kill the aggressor in the process (#'s 2258–2264).

2. Those responsible for the lives of others must defend the common good and stop unjust aggressors by force of arms if necessary (#2265).

3. The state can punish people in ways appropriate to the seriousness of their crime in order to protect the public order and people's safety and to correct the guilty people. Non-lethal forms of punishment should be used; the need for the death penalty is practically nonexistent today (#'s 2266–2267).

B. Peace

1. Respect for human life requires peace, which is more than the absence of war or a balance of powers. It requires protection of people's goods, open communication, respect for human dignity, and community. It results from justice and charity (#2304).

2. The Peace of Christ is built upon the reconciliation of all with each other and with God; the Church is to be a sign of the unity intended for the whole human community (#2305).

3. Those who choose non-violent approaches to protecting human rights give valuable witness to the danger of relying on violence (#2306).

C. Avoiding War

1. All should pray that God free the human community of war and work to avoid it. If war is an imminent danger and there is no adequate international authority, governments may defend themselves as a last resort (#'s 2307–2308).

2. There are strict conditions for legitimate military defense that must be considered by those responsible for the common good:
   a. There must be danger of "lasting, grave, and certain" damage.
   b. It is a last resort.
   c. There must be serious prospects of success.
   d. And the result of the war must not be worse that the evil being prevented (#2309).

3. The state can require military service for national defense but must make provision for conscientious objectors to serve the common good in another way (#'s 2310–2311).

4. The moral law must be observed in the way the war is carried on, including by treating non-combatants, wounded soldiers, and prisoners humanely (#'s 2312–2313).

5. Acts of war aimed at genocide, ethnic cleansing, indiscriminate destruction of whole cities, or vast areas are crimes against God and humanity and must be resisted (#'s 2313–2314).

6. The arms race does not deter aggressors or ensure peace. Arms spending steals from the poor, thwarts development, and risks more conflict. Production and sale of arms can serve the common good and should be regulated by public authorities so that they don't serve violence and conflict (#'s 2315–2316).

7. To build peace and avoid war, injustice, excessive economic or social inequalities, envy, distrust, and pride must be overcome (#2317).

IV. Miscellaneous Topics: Justice, the Church, and Hunger

1. The virtue of Justice is the firm will to give God and neighbor their due. It respects the rights of each and works for harmonious human relationships and the common good (#1807).

2. The Church makes moral judgments in political matters when necessary for human rights or people's salvation and invites

public officials to consider them. It respects political freedom and citizen responsibility (#'s 2244–2246).

3. In the prayer Jesus gave us, Christians pray, "Give us this day our daily bread." In the face of world hunger, Christians must work to establish just social, economic international relations so that the spiritual and material needs of all can be met through solidarity with all their brothers and sisters (#'s 2831–2833).

16

THE GOSPEL OF LIFE

Evangelium Vitae, Encyclical Letter of Pope John Paul II, 1995

Major Areas of Concern
—Conscience Formation
—Human Dignity and Life
—Abortion
—Euthanasia
—Death Penalty
—Conscientious Objection

In *The Gospel of Life,* Pope John Paul II rallies against "the culture of death," and urges a "new culture of human life" that affirms the dignity and inviolability of all human life. The encyclical begins by reflecting on the threats to life including abortion, euthanasia, poverty, hunger, violence, and war. He then sketches a "Gospel of Life" that flows from the Old Testament commandment "You shall not kill" and the New Testament commandment "Love one another." This personal and passionate letter concludes with the Pope commissioning various ministries in the Church to spread this gospel of life.

HISTORICAL NOTE

Pope John Paul II published this encyclical in 1995 in response to a multitude of threats to life that he considers to be rampant at the dawn of the third millennium. The letter gives voice to several key themes of his papacy as expressed in various journeys throughout the world. *The Gospel of Life* affirms the "Consistent Ethic of Life" developed by the late Joseph Cardinal Bernardin of Chicago.

Introduction

1. Life is a sacred reality meant to be brought to perfection by humans in love (#2).
2. Every human and political community is founded on the value of life (#2).
3. Extraordinary threats to "weak and defenseless" life exist including "poverty, hunger, endemic diseases, violence and war" (#3).
4. "A new cultural climate is developing" that is influencing public opinion to "justify certain crimes against life" (#4).
5. Not only are human lives being destroyed but individual and social consciences are finding it "difficult to distinguish between good and evil" (#4).
6. "Justice, development, true freedom, peace and happiness" rest on the foundation of the dignity of human life (#5).
7. A "new culture of human life" is needed to build "an authentic civilization of truth and love" (#6).

I. Threats to Human Life

1. A lack of solidarity, lies, and evasions of responsibility are all threats to human life (#8).
2. Threats to life include murder, war, genocide, poverty, hunger, malnutrition, "an unjust distribution of resources," "the scandalous arms trade," "reckless tampering with the world's ecological balance," "the criminal spread of drugs," and "the profound crisis of culture" (#'s 10–11).
3. Human life is threatened by the "culture of death" which is "a veritable structure of sin" and "a war of the powerful against the weak" (#12).
4. Despite being of different moral seriousness, contraception and abortion are often both rooted in sexual irresponsibility and a self-centered concept of freedom (#13).
5. "Various techniques of artificial reproduction . . . actually open the door to threats against life" (#14).
6. Euthanasia is justified by both "misguided pity" and a "utilitarian motive of avoiding costs which bring no return and which weigh heavily on society" (#15).

7. "Rich and developed countries" continue to enact "anti-birth policies" for the "poorer countries" instead of "programs of cultural development and of fair production and distribution of resources"(#16).

8. "The twentieth century will have been an era of massive attacks on life" (#17).

9. Social and political problems, as well as a misguided understanding of rights, trample upon the right to life (#18).

10. The culture of death "betrays a completely individualistic concept of freedom" (#19).

11. By not respecting life, the State "is transformed into a tyrant State, which arrogates to itself the right to dispose of the weakest and most defenseless members" (#20).

12. The heart of the tragedy is "the eclipse of the sense of God" and humanity (#21).

13. This eclipse "leads to a practical materialism which breeds individualism, utilitarianism, and hedonism" (#23).

14. The human body "is reduced to pure materiality . . . a complex of organs" (#23).

15. The culture of sin creates and consolidates "actual structures of sin" (#24).

16. Positive "signs of hope" exist in our world including families, volunteers, advances in medical science, agencies and organizations, and a "growing solidarity among peoples" (#26).

17. Other signs include an increased sensitivity in opposition to war as an instrument of conflict resolution, increased opposition to the death penalty, "growing attention to ecology," and "more widespread development of bioethics" (#27).

18. Faith is the biggest help to choosing life (#28).

II. The Christian Message of Life

1. The Gospel of Life is "concrete and personal" (#29).

2. "The fullness of the Gospel message about life was prepared for in the Old Testament" (#31).

3. Jesus teaches the poor, sick, and the outcast that their lives have "great value" (#32).

4. In Jesus, there is a "singular dialectic" between "the uncertainty of human life and the affirmation of its value" (#33).

5. The dignity of human life is linked to both its origin and destiny in God and God's love (#38).

6. "Human life is in the hands of God . . . like those of a mother who accepts, nurtures and takes care of her child" (#39).

7. There is a "requirement to show reverence and love for . . . the life of every person" (#41).

8. Human beings have "a specific responsibility towards the environment . . . not only for the present but also for future generations" (#42).

9. Human beings are made in the image and likeness of God as "co-workers with God" (#43).

III. "You Shall Not Kill: God's Holy Law"

1. "The Gospel of life is both a great gift of God and an exacting task for humanity" (#52).

2. "Human life is sacred because from the beginning it involves 'the creative action of God'" (#53).

3. "'You shall not kill' . . . encourages a positive attitude of absolute respect for life" (#54).

4. The only justification for the death penalty is "absolute necessity . . . when it would not be possible otherwise to defend society. . . . Such cases are very rare, if not practically non-existent" (#56).

5. Given "the progressive weakening in individual consciences and in society . . . the Church's Magisterium has spoken out with increasing frequency in defense of the sacredness and inviolability of human life" (#57).

6. "Abortion goes beyond the responsibility of individuals . . . and takes on a distinctly social dimension" in the institutions and networks that protect and promote it (#'s 58–59).

7. "Euthanasia is a grave violation of the law of God, since it is the deliberate and morally unacceptable killing of a human person" (#65).

8. "True 'compassion' leads to sharing another's pain; it does not kill the person whose suffering we cannot bear" (#66).

9. Democracy does not require moral relativism; it cannot substitute for morality (#70).

10. "An almost universal consensus with regard to the value of democracy . . . is to be considered a positive 'sign of the times'" (#70). But care must be taken to prevent the most powerful from manipulating participatory processes to serve their own interests.

11. "Laws which authorize and promote abortion and euthanasia are . . . radically opposed not only to the good of the individual but also to the common good" (#72).

12. "There is no obligation in conscience to obey such laws; instead there is a grave and clear obligation to oppose them by conscientious objection" (#73).

13. "'You shall not kill' . . . involves an absolute imperative to respect, love, and promote the life of every brother and sister" (#77).

IV. A New Culture of Human Life

1. "We need to bring the Gospel of life to the heart of every man and woman and to make it penetrate every part of society" (#80).
2. "Society as a whole must respect, defend and promote the dignity of every human person, at every moment and in every condition of that person's life" (#81).
3. "In celebrating the Gospel of life we also need to appreciate and make good use of the wealth of gestures and symbols present in the traditions and customs of different cultures and peoples" (#85).
4. "Social activity and political commitment" are ways to support and promote human life (#87).
5. Political leaders need to make attainable choices that "will lead to the re-establishment of a just order in the defense and promotion of the value of life" (#90).
6. "Special attention must be given the elderly" (#94).
7. "The first and fundamental step towards this cultural transformation consists in forming consciences with regard to the incomparable and inviolable worth of every human life" (#96).

17

CONTRIBUTION TO WORLD CONFERENCE AGAINST RACISM, RACIAL DISCRIMINATION, XENOPHOBIA AND RELATED INTOLERANCE

Pontifical Council for Justice and Peace, 2001

Major Areas of Concern
—Racism
—Discrimination
—National Reconciliation
—Development
—Education
—Affirmative Action
—Freedom of Conscience

The *Contribution* begins by noting an increase in racism and discrimination in the thirteen years since the Pontifical Council for Justice and Peace published *The Church and Racism*. The *Contribution* emphasizes the importance of the Church's appeal for personal conversion, and the necessity of requesting and granting pardons for past actions. The document stresses the importance of education in combating racism and the teaching of values such as human dignity and unity in promoting solidarity and the common good. The *Contribution* concludes by highlighting the importance of freedom of conscience and religion.

HISTORICAL NOTE

The Pontifical Council for Justice and Peace used the opportunity of a major world conference on racism held in Durban, South Africa, in 2001 to republish its 1988 document, *The Church and Racism,* and issue this corollary. The *Contribution* cites extensively a number of interventions and addresses by Pope John Paul II. The document places a special emphasis on actions the Pope had taken in the Jubilee Year of 2000 to request pardon for Church actions or omissions that may have contributed to racism and discrimination.

A. **The Increase of Racism**
1. With the acceleration of globalization and the escalation of ethnic violence, racism has increased since 1988 (#'s 1–4).
2. "It is right to rejoice at the end of the apartheid regime in South Africa" (#4).
3. "While the law may have abolished slavery everywhere, the practice still persists, notably in Africa among people of different ethnic groups" (#4).

B. **The Catholic Church's Appeal for Conversion**
1. "The contribution of the Catholic Church, in its constant appeal for personal conversion, is most important and necessary" (#5).
2. "Christians in particular have the responsibility to offer a teaching that stresses the dignity of every human being and the unity of the human race" (#5).
3. In the Jubilee Year of 2000, Pope John Paul II issued a solemn request for "pardon for past acts and omissions of the Church which may have encouraged and/or perpetuated discrimination against particular groups of people" (#6).
4. After pardon is granted, "a 'purification of memory' then becomes necessary" (#6).
5. "This occurs whenever it becomes possible to attribute to past historical deeds a different quality, having a new and different effect on the present, in view of the progress in reconciliation in truth, justice and charity among human beings" (#6).
6. During the Jubilee Year, the Pope requested pardon for "faults committed in relations with the people of Israel . . . against the

dignity of women . . . [from] the peoples of Africa for the slave trade . . . [and from] the American Indians and Africans deported as slaves" (#7).

C. Pardon and National Reconciliation

1. The Church "hopes that political leaders and peoples, especially those involved in tragic conflicts, fueled by hatred and the memory of often ancient wounds, will be guided by the spirit of forgiveness and reconciliation exemplified by the Church" (#8).

2. Conditional amnesty and "truth and reconciliation commissions" can assist nations which have been "destroyed and divided by serious conflicts" to engage in reconciliation (#8).

3. "The weight of history, with its litany of resentments, fears, suspicions between families, ethnic groups or populations must first be overcome" (#9).

4. "Local Churches have an active role to play, notably through their messages of forgiveness and reconciliation" (#10).

5. "All forms of mediation therefore should be encouraged" (#10).

6. "Forgiveness has its own demands: the evil which has been done must be acknowledged and, as far as possible, corrected" (#11).

7. The "primary demands" of forgiveness are respect for truth and justice (#11).

8. "The duty to make reparation must be fulfilled . . . reparation should erase all the consequences of the illicit action and restore things to the way they would most probably be" (#12).

9. "The need for reparation reinforces the obligation of giving substantial help to developing countries, an obligation weighing chiefly on the more developed countries" (#12).

D. Education Against Racism and Discrimination

1. "The roots of racism, discrimination and intolerance are found in prejudice and ignorance, which are first of all the fruits of sin, but also of faulty and inadequate education" (#13).

2. "All people of whatever race, condition or age, in virtue of their dignity as human persons have an inalienable right to education" (#13).

3. "Education is a matter of teaching the human being to become 'ever more human,' to 'be more' rather than to 'have more' . . . to 'be with others' but even more to 'be for others'" (#14).

4. Education should emphasize "certain major values such as the unity of the human race, the dignity of every human being, the solidarity which binds together all the members of the human family [and] . . . respect for human rights" (#15).

    5. The media has a duty to promote "the common good" (#16).

    6. Religions "must show that religious belief inspires peace, encourages solidarity, promotes justice and upholds liberty" (#17).

E. Affirmative Action

    1. "These voluntary measures are intended to ensure effective recognition of the equality of all, for example by facilitating access to bank loans for a particular category of the population" (#18).

    2. "The choice of this kind of policy remains controversial. There is a real risk that such measures will crystallize differences rather than foster social cohesion" (#19).

    3. Affirmative action "must be temporary . . . ought not to have the effect of maintaining different rights for different groups and . . . must not be kept in force once their objectives have been achieved" (#19).

F. Immigrants, Poverty and Discrimination

    1. Everyone should "be generous in their welcome . . . and recognize that immigrants bring with them the riches of their culture, history and traditions" (#20).

    2. "The Local Churches . . . have not hesitated to enter into public debate in order to condemn racism and foster openness to immigrants" (#20).

    3. "Since 1988, two great global divides have grown deeper: the first is the ever more tragic phenomenon of poverty and social discrimination and the other, more recent and less widely condemned, concerns the unborn child" (#21).

    4. "Freedom of conscience and freedom of religion remain the premise, the principle and the foundation of every other freedom, human and civil, individual and communal" (#22).

PART THREE

DOCUMENTS TO THE REGIONAL CHURCHES

Introduction

In 1971, Pope Paul VI issued *A Call to Action (Octogesima Adveniens)* in which he wrote:

> In the face of such widely varying situations it is difficult for us to utter a unified message and to put forward a solution which has universal validity. Such is not our ambition, nor is it our mission. It is up to the Christian communities to analyze with objectivity the situation which is proper to their own country, to shed on it the light of the Gospel's unalterable words and to draw principles of reflection, norms of judgment and directives for action from the social teaching of the church. (#4)

This section of *Catholic Social Teaching: Our Best Kept Secret* presents outlines of nineteen documents from six regions of the world that have emerged as responses to this important call to action.

These regional documents build upon the documents to the universal Church and develop them. They reveal an increasing recognition in the Church of cultural, geographic and historical differences, and they witness to the growing importance of local and regional church statements. Reading the texts will show that while the documents are directed to regional situations and audiences, their implications reach beyond those boundaries. They are addressing common problems of globalization faced by governments and those in poverty in many parts of the world.

These documents have been issued by regional conferences of bishops. Two of them, however, stand out because of the unique process through which they were developed. *The Challenge of Peace: God's Promise and Our Response* and *Economic Justice for All: Catholic Social Teaching and the U.S. Economy* were each the subject of extensive public discussion over a period of years in the most participatory process of Church discernment and teaching ever attempted. A first draft of each was published, and then the extensive public dialogue and feedback shaped revisions and subsequent drafts until the bishops finalized the text and promulgated it formally.

As the Church's social teaching continues to develop, local statements such as these will assume ever greater importance. They may one day form part of a process through which the teachings of local churches will be gathered to form teachings that are *from* as well as *to* the universal Church.

18

Brothers and Sisters to Us

Pastoral Letter of the United States Bishops, 1979

```
Major Areas of Concern
—Racism
—Employment
—Conversion
—Working Conditions
—Distribution of Resources
```

The pastoral begins by calling racism a sin and an evil. It explores ways in which racism has been manifested—both in the past and at present—in the Church and in society. The bishops state that all people are created in the image of God and should be treated with corresponding dignity. The pastoral concludes with a sketch of a plan for combating racism on the individual, Church, national, and international levels.

HISTORICAL NOTE

Brothers and Sisters to Us is the third major pastoral statement in which the U.S. bishops attack racism. The other two appeared in 1958 and 1968. This letter was an initial response to the consultation on social justice which formed part of "A Call to Action," one of the vehicles for U.S. Catholic participation in the 1976 U.S. Bicentennial.

Introduction

1. "Racism is an evil which endures in our society and in our Church."
2. Most Americans think racism is unjust and unworthy of the U.S.
3. Racism and economic oppression are related.

The Sin of Racism

1. Racism is a sin that divides the human family and violates human dignity.
2. In the U.S. people are denied opportunities because of race.

Racism Is a Fact

1. Unemployment figures, education and housing statistics, and prison censuses all point to racism in the U.S.

A Look at the Past

1. Slavery, economic exploitation, and cultural repression are part of the racist fabric of U.S. history.

Racism Today

1. Racism is also manifested today in:
   a. a sense of indifference to the marginalized;
   b. the triumph of the individual and success over social commitment and compassion.

God's Judgment and Promise

1. God's word proclaims:
   a. all men and women are created in God's image;
   b. the liberation of all people from slavery.
2. Racism is "a distortion at the very heart of human nature."
3. The Church and individual Catholics must:
   a. acknowledge past mistakes and sins;
   b. prophetically strive for racial justice and human dignity.

Our Response: Our Personal Lives

1. Conversion and renewal are necessary.
2. Individuals need to:

    a. reject racial stereotypes and racist jokes;

    b. learn more about and work for just social structures.

Our Response: Our Church Community

1. The Church must examine its behavior toward minorities.
2. Among the actions the Church needs to take vis-à-vis minorities are:
   a. foster vocations;
   b. increase representation in the hierarchy;
   c. provide just conditions for employment;
   d. care for undocumented workers;
   e. provide leadership training programs;
   f. support minority associations;
   g. continue and expand inner city Catholic schools.

Our Response: Society at Large

1. Domestically, we need to strive for full employment and just working conditions.
2. Internationally, we need to promote racial justice and a just distribution of resources.

Conclusion

1. We must not turn back, but must push ahead, on the road to racial justice.

19

THE CHALLENGE OF PEACE: GOD'S PROMISE AND OUR RESPONSE

Pastoral Letter of the United States Bishops, 1983

Major Areas of Concern
—Just War
—Non-violence
—Theology of Peace
—Nuclear War
—Deterrence
—Arms Control
—Conflict Resolution
—World Order

The pastoral begins with a preliminary sketch of a theology of peace, building on scriptures and the Catholic just war and non-violent traditions. It moves to a critical discussion of the use of nuclear weapons and the policy of deterrence. The Bishops then propose a number of steps for arms control and conflict resolution. The letter concludes with the Bishops articulating a pastoral response for the Church as it grapples with the issues of war and peace.

HISTORICAL NOTE

The pastoral letter was written by an ad hoc committee of five Bishops chaired by Joseph Cardinal Bernardin. The committee consulted widely among theologians, defense experts, and government officials. The pastoral, heavily influenced by *The Church in the Modern World* and the teachings of Pope John Paul II, went through three drafts before being approved by the National Conference of Catholic Bishops meeting in special session in Chicago in 1983.

Introduction

1. Faith should intensify our desire to tackle the challenges of life (#2).
2. Nuclear war is a more menacing challenge than any the world has ever faced (#3).
3. Letter is invitation and challenge to shape policies in this "moment of supreme crisis" (#4).

I. Religious Perspectives on Peace

1. "The nuclear threat transcends religious, cultural, and national boundaries" (#6).
2. *The Church in the Modern World* provided the Bishops with guidelines for their statements (#7).
3. Different statements in the pastoral carry different levels of authority (#'s 9–11).
4. Three "signs of the times" influence us: world wants peace, arms race is a curse, and new problems call for fresh approach (#13).
5. Two purposes of Catholic teaching on peace and war: inform consciences and contribute to policy debate (#16).
6. Need for a "theology of peace" which is biblical, pastoral, hopeful (#25).

A. Peace and the Kingdom
1. In the Old Testament:
   a. Metaphor of the warrior God was gradually reformed after the Exile (#31).
   b. Peace is understood in a variety of ways (#32):
      i. is a gift of God's saving activity;
      ii. pertains to the unity and harmony of community;
      iii. demands covenantal fidelity of the people to true peace.
   c. Fidelity to God, justice, and peace are all connected (#35).

    d. Messianic time offered hope for the eschatological peace (#36).

  2. In the New Testament:

    a. Image of warrior God disappears (#40).

    b. Jesus proclaims God's reign of love and God's gift of peace (#'s 47, 51).

    c. Jesus in his death and resurrection gives God's peace to the world (#54).

B. Kingdom and History

  1. Christian view of history is hopeful and calls for a peace based on justice (#56).

  2. Bishops are convinced "peace is possible" (#59).

C. Moral Choices for the Kingdom

  1. Need to undertake a "completely fresh reappraisal of war" (*Peace on Earth*) (#66).

  2. "Peace is both a gift of God and a human work" (#68).

  3. In a spirit of love the Christian must defend peace, properly understood, against aggression (#'s 73–78).

  4. Just-war criteria attempt to prevent war and limit the conditions that will allow war to happen (#'s 81–84).

    a. *Jus ad Bellum* (why and when war):

      i. just cause—only a real and certain danger (#86);

      ii. competent authority—declared by legitimately responsible public officials (#'s 87–88);

      iii. comparative justice—rights and values involved justify killing (#92);

      iv. right intention—pursuit of peace and reconciliation (#95);

      v. last resort—all peaceful alternatives exhausted (#96);

      vi. probability of success (#98);

      vii. proportionality—damage to be inflicted must be proportionate to the good expected (#99).

    b. *Jus in Bello* (how war is to be conducted):

      i. proportionality—response to the aggression must not exceed the nature of the aggression (#'s 103, 105–106);

      ii. discrimination—not directed against innocent non-combatants (#'s 104, 107).

  5. Non-violent commitment:

    a. has rich history in Christian tradition (#'s 111–115);

    b. is not passive about injustice (#116);

    c. includes conscientious and selective conscientious objection (#118);

    d. is stressed as legitimate option for Christian (#119);

  e. is interdependent with just-war teaching in common pre-
     sumption against force (#120).

II. War and Peace in the Modern World

A. The New Moment
   1. Arms race condemned as dangerous, folly, a crime against the
      poor (#128).
   2. "No" to nuclear war must be definitive and decisive (#138).

B. Religious Leadership
   1. As moral teachers, we must resist idea of nuclear war as instru-
      ment to national policy (#139).
   2. We must shape public opinion against rhetoric about winning
      nuclear war (#140).

C. Use of Nuclear Weapons
   1. "Under no circumstances" may nuclear weapons be used
      against civilian population centers (#147).
   2. The initiation of nuclear war is not morally justifiable (#'s 150–
      153).
   3. Bishops are "highly skeptical" about the moral acceptability of
      a limited nuclear war (#'s 157–161).

D. Deterrence
   1. Vatican II and U.S. Catholic Conference statements have weighed
      deterrence policy benefits (possible prevention of nuclear war)
      and dangers (escalation of arms race, cost inflicted on poor)
      (#'s 167–170).
   2. Pope John Paul II concludes deterrence may be "morally
      acceptable" as a step toward progressive disarmament
      (#173).
   3. Deterrence:
      a. is never morally acceptable when it threatens to kill the
         innocent (#178);
      b. should not result in strategies for fighting wars (#184).
   4. The Bishops give a "strictly conditioned moral acceptance" of
      nuclear deterrence (#186).
      a. No acceptance of "prevailing" in nuclear war (#188).
      b. "Sufficiency" not "superiority" must be goal (#188).
      c. Every new system must be assessed as a step toward "pro-
         gressive disarmament" (#188).
   5. Bishops oppose "first strike" weapons and lowering of nuclear
      threshold (#190).
   6. Bishops recommend bilateral, verifiable "halt" to new systems;
      bilateral deep cuts in superpower arsenals; comprehensive test
      ban treaty (#191).

7. Deterrence policy must be scrutinized with greatest care in ongoing public debate on moral grounds (#195).
8. Bishops acknowledge that many strong voices in the Catholic community reject deterrence and call for a prophetic challenge to take steps for peace (#'s 197–198).

III. The Promotion of Peace

A. Specific Steps

1. The U.S. should take initiative in reduction and disarmament action including:
   a. continual negotiation with potential adversaries (#207);
   b. support for nuclear non-proliferation (#208).
2. The world should:
   a. ban chemical and biological weapons (#210);
   b. control arms exports (#'s 211–213).
3. Conventional forces must also be reduced (#'s 216–218).
4. Civil defense must be examined to see if it is realistic in light of a possible nuclear attack (#220).
5. We must find ways other than force to defend nation's citizens and values (#221).
   a. Non-violent resistance and popular defense need more study (#'s 222–227).
   b. Peace research, conflict resolution studies, peace education programs, U.S. Peace Academy are all endorsed (#'s 228–230).
6. While military service may be required, rights of conscientious and selective conscientious objection must be respected by law (#'s 232–233).

B. Shaping a Peaceful World

1. Peace is not simply absence of war, but presence of justice (#234).
2. Unity of human family and a just world order are central to Catholic social teaching (#'s 235–244).
3. While Americans should have no illusions about the Soviet government, it is in the interest of both superpowers to work for peace, going beyond stereotypes or hardened positions (#'s 245–258).
4. The realization of the world's growing interdependence should lead the U.S. to:
   a. promote structural reform to aid the world's poor (#264);
   b. support reform to make U.N. more effective (#268);
   c. reverse the arms race to make needed resources available for development (#270).

IV. The Pastoral Challenge and Response

A. The Church
　1. "To be disciples of Jesus requires that we continually go beyond where we now are" (#276).
　2. The Christian must take a stand against much of what the world accepts as right (#277).

B. Pastoral Response
　1. Church should develop balanced educational programs about peace, respecting legitimate differences (#'s 280–283).
　2. True peace demands a reverence for life, rejection of violence, and an end to abortion (#'s 284–289).
　3. Personal and communal prayer is helpful for fostering conversion of hearts (#290).
　4. Optional Friday fast and abstinence are tangible signs of penance for peace (#298).

C. Challenge and Hope
　1. We must shape climate to make it possible to express sorrow for atomic bombing in 1945 (#302).
　2. Many different sectors of American society—including priests and religious, parents and youth, public officials and military personnel—have special requirements to promote peace (#'s 301–327).

Conclusion

　1. The Bishops speak as pastors, trying to live up to the call of Jesus to be peacemakers (#331).
　2. We need "moral about-face" to say "no" to nuclear war and arms race (#333).
　3. The risen Christ helps us confront the challenge of nuclear arms race with trust in God's power (#339).

20

THE HISPANIC PRESENCE: CHALLENGE AND COMMITMENT

Pastoral Letter of the United States Bishops, 1984

Major Areas of Concern
—Hispanic Situation
—Pastoral Ministry
—Human Dignity
—Poverty
—Political Participation
—Option for the Poor
—Families

The pastoral begins by focusing on the reality of Hispanics in the United States. The bishops consider the increase in the number of Hispanics a "pastoral opportunity." The bishops then enumerate the pastoral implications of this fact. They call for a wide range of responses involving all Catholics. The pastoral concludes by articulating the bishops' commitment to Hispanic ministry.

HISTORICAL NOTE

The Hispanic Presence is the first pastoral letter of the U.S. bishops exclusively on Hispanic ministry. Pastoral letters focusing on Hispanic ministry were written in 1982 by the U.S. Hispanic bishops and the Santa Fe province bishops. The U.S. bishops' pastoral sought to respond to the needs of the then-20 million U.S. Hispanics. (The number of U.S. Hispanics continues to increase significantly.) The bishops followed this pastoral letter with a pastoral plan published in 1987.

I. A Call to Hispanic Ministry

1. The Hispanic community in the U.S. is a "blessing from God" (#1).
2. Hispanics want more opportunities to share their gifts with the Church (#2).
3. Hispanics exemplify and cherish values such as human dignity, family, community, and devotion to Mary (#3).
4. The increase in the number of Hispanics in the U.S. is a pastoral opportunity (#4).
5. More than 85 percent of Hispanics live in urban centers (#6).
6. In the U.S., most Hispanics live near or below the poverty level (#7).
7. Hispanics are "severely underrepresented" at society's and the Church's decision-making levels (#7).
8. Unemployment and a lack of educational opportunities hurt Hispanics (#7).

II. Achievements in Hispanic Ministry in U.S.

1. Hispanic women have nurtured the faith in their families and communities (#9).
2. The large number of Hispanic lay leaders and permanent deacons is a healthy sign (#9).
3. A number of apostolic movements, such as Cursillos and Encuentros, are also noteworthy (#9).
4. The appointments of Hispanic bishops and archbishops are also positive signs (#9).

III. Urgent Pastoral Implications

1. All Catholics should respond to the Hispanic presence (#10).
2. Both the sense of the faithful and hierarchical teachings are important in Hispanic ministry (#11).
3. Liturgy and preaching should be in Spanish and/or bilingual when appropriate (#12).
4. Enrolling in Spanish classes is "strongly recommended" for priests and chaplains (#12).

5. Vocations to lay, clerical, and religious life should be encouraged (#12).
6. Catholic schools should form and become an advocate for their students (#12).
7. Hispanic issues need better coverage in the Catholic media (#12).
8. Catholics must live the Gospel "more authentically" to respond to the fundamentalist challenge (#12).
9. Ministry should respond to the needs of Hispanic youth and families (#12).
10. Treatment of migrants and undocumented workers is "deplorable"; the Church supports their rights (#12).
11. The Church and Hispanics need to increase their work for social justice (#12).
12. The Church advocates an end to the racism and prejudice that causes "pervasive poverty" for Hispanics (#12).
13. The U.S. Church will support and assist the Latin American Church (#12).
14. Closer dialogue between popular and official pastoral practice is needed (#12).
15. The development of Basic Christian Communities is "highly encouraged" (#12).

IV. Statement of Commitment

1. The Church is both pluralistic and unified (#14).
2. Catholics should develop a "more welcoming attitude" toward Hispanics (#14).
3. The Bishops will defend the human dignity of Hispanics (#15).
4. All Catholics should deepen their "preferential option for the poor" by fostering Hispanic political participation (#15).
5. The Bishops pledge to devote financial and material resources to Hispanic ministry (#17).
6. The Bishops promise to draft a pastoral plan for Hispanic ministry (#18).
7. The Bishops envision a "new era" of Hispanic ministry (#20).

21

Economic Justice for All: Catholic Social Teaching and the U.S. Economy

Pastoral Letter of the United States Bishops, 1986

Major Areas of Concern
—Biblical Justice
—Option for the Poor
—Participation
—Economic Rights
—Employment
—Poverty
—Agriculture
—Global Economy

Economic Justice for All attempts to apply the major principles of Catholic social teaching to the structure of the U.S. economy. The Bishops write to provide moral perspective on the economy and to assess the economy's impact on the poor. The Bishops begin their letter with a description of the economy today and develop a moral vision, based on biblical teachings and the tradition of Catholic social thought, of a just economy. They then apply this vision to several policy areas: employment, poverty, agriculture, and international development. They end by calling for cooperation in a "New American Experiment" and a commitment by all sectors of the economy to a future of solidarity.

HISTORICAL NOTE

The U.S. Bishops issued this pastoral letter on the economy in 1986, three and one-half years after their Peace Pastoral. In drafting the letter, the Bishops consulted widely among business leaders, academicians, government officials, and other segments of American society, as well as among theologians and Church leaders. They held several hearings at various locations throughout the United States and received almost twenty thousand written suggestions as they circulated three preliminary drafts. The pastoral is significantly influenced by Vatican II's call to read the "signs of the times," the social teaching of the Council, and the social teachings of Pope John Paul II.

I. The Church and the Future of the U.S. Economy

1. Three questions to shape economic perspective (#1):
   a. What does the economy do *for* people?
   b. What does it do *to* people?
   c. How do people *participate* in it?
2. U.S. economy has many successes but also many failures (#'s 2–3).

A. U.S. Economy Today: Memory and Hope

1. U.S. has high standard of living, productive work, vast natural resources (#6).
2. Economy has involved serious conflict and suffering, and has been built through creative struggle of many (#'s 7–8).

B. Urgent Problems

1. Sign of the times: Preeminent role of U.S. in increasingly interdependent global economy (#10).
2. Mobility of capital and technology affects jobs worldwide (#11).
3. Pollution and depletion of resources threaten environment (#12).
4. Promise of American dream remains unfulfilled for millions in U.S., with high unemployment and harsh poverty (#'s 14–16).
5. Economic life does not support family life (#18).
6. Investment of so many resources into production of weapons increases the problems (#20).
7. Culture/value questions are a deeper challenge to the nation (#21).

C. The Need for Moral Vision

1. Service of the poor: fundamental criterion of economic policy (#24).
2. Pastoral based on Catholic social thought tradition that honors human dignity in community with others and whole of creation (#'s 32–34).
3. Bishops write to (#27):
   a. provide guidance for formation of Catholic consciences;
   b. add voice to public debate on direction of the economy.

II. The Christian Vision of Economic Life

Economic life is to support and serve human dignity (#28).

A. Biblical Perspectives

1. Humans are created in God's image, possess intrinsic dignity, and enjoy gift of creation (#'s 32–34).
2. God's covenant with Israel calls for loving justice which promotes human dignity (#'s 35–40).
3. Jesus proclaims compassion and call to discipleship (#'s 43–47).
4. The preferential option for the poor calls the church "to see things from the side of the poor" (#52).
5. Action for justice proceeds from hope and emphasizes new creation (#'s 54–55).
6. Catholic life and thought about economics are enriched through history and learn from other traditions (#'s 56–59).
7. Concerns of letter are central, integral to proclamation of Gospel (#60).

B. Ethical Norms for Economic Life

1. Responsibilities of social living include:
   a. active love of God and neighbor which makes human solidarity and community possible (#'s 64, 66);
   b. establishment of minimum levels of commutative, distributive, and social justice and institutions that support justice (#'s 68–73);
   c. examination of inequalities of income, consumption, privilege, and power (#'s 74–76);
   d. establishment of minimum levels of participation in social institutions (#'s 77–78).
2. Human rights must be respected which:
   a. promote the common good (#79);
   b. include political-civil and social-economic rights as outlined in John XXIII's *Peace on Earth* (#80);
   c. enhance and reflect just institutions (#82);
   d. embody new cultural consensus in U.S. (#'s 83–84).

3. Poor have the single most urgent claim on conscience of nation (#86).
4. U.S. moral priorities should be:
   a. fulfillment of basic needs of the poor (#90);
   b. active participation in economic life by those now excluded (#91);
   c. investment of wealth, talent, and energy for benefit of poor (#92);
   d. strengthening of family life (#93).

C. Working for Greater Justice

1. Through daily work people make their largest contribution to economic justice (#96).
2. Threefold moral significance of work (#97):
   a. principal way for self-expression and creativity;
   b. ordinary way to fulfill material needs;
   c. way to contribute to the larger community.
3. Principle of subsidiarity gives everyone the task of working for justice (#'s 98–99).
4. Workers' right to organize must be respected; just and vital labor unions contribute to the economy's future (#'s 102–109).
5. Business people, managers, owners have a vocation to serve the common good (#'s 110–111).
6. Private property is always at service of common good, and is limited by a "social mortgage" (#'s 114–115).
7. Every citizen has the responsibility to work with others for justice (#120).
8. Government, respecting "subsidiarity," should help groups seeking to promote the common good (#124).

III. Selected Economic Policy Issues

Introduction

1. Church is not bound to any particular economic, political, or social system, but asks: What is impact on people (#130).
2. Our approach is pragmatic and evolutionary, accepting "mixed" economic system and urging its reform to be more just (#131).
3. But larger systemic questions do need to be asked about our economy and its values (#132).

A. Employment

1. Most urgent priority for domestic policy is creation of new jobs with adequate pay and decent working conditions (#136).
2. Unemployment affects eight million people, disproportionately blacks, Hispanics, youth, at severe human costs (#'s 138–142).

3. Current levels of unemployment, assaulting human dignity, are intolerable (#143).
4. Demographic changes, advancing technology, global competition, discrimination, and increased defense spending all have driven up rate of unemployment (#'s 144–149).
5. The U.S. should:
    a. establish consensus that everyone has a right to employment (#153);
    b. coordinate fiscal and monetary policy to achieve full employment (#156);
    c. expand private sector job-training, especially for the long-term unemployed, to establish more socially useful jobs (#'s 156–165);
    d. explore new strategies to improve the quantity and quality of jobs (#'s 167–168).

B. Poverty

1. Poverty, affecting 33 million Americans and dramatically increasing, is "lack of sufficient material resources required for a decent life" (#'s 170–173).
2. Characteristics of today's poverty include:
    a. growing number of children, especially minorities (#'s 176–177);
    b. increasing number of women and female-headed families (#'s 178–180);
    c. disproportionate number of minorities (#'s 181–182).
3. Great inequality in distribution of wealth and income in U.S. affects power and participation and is "unacceptable" (#'s 183–185).
4. Alleviation of poverty in U.S. will require:
    a. fundamental changes in social and economic structures (#187);
    b. programs which empower the poor to help themselves (#188);
    c. doing away with stereotypes that stigmatize the poor (#'s 193–194).
5. Elements of national strategy to deal with poverty include:
    a. sustain an economy that provides just wages for all adults able to work (#'s 196–197);
    b. remove barriers to equal employment for women and minorities (#199);
    c. foster "self-help" programs for the poor (#'s 200–201);
    d. evaluate tax system in terms of impact on the poor (#202);
    e. make a stronger commitment to education for the poor in public and private schools (#'s 203–205);

f. promote policies which support and strengthen families (#'s 206–209);

g. reform the welfare system so it respects human dignity (#'s 210–214).

C. Food and Agriculture

1. Increased concentration of land ownership and depletion of natural resources threaten farm life (#217).

2. Structures of U.S. agriculture, affected by new technologies and export orientation, have led to trend of fewer and larger farms (#'s 220–223).

3. Diversity and richness in American society are lost with exodus from rural areas; minorities especially suffer (#'s 225, 229–230).

4. Guidelines for action include:

    a. protect moderate-sized, family-operated farms (#'s 233–235);

    b. safeguard the opportunity to engage in farming (#'s 236–237);

    c. provide stewardship for natural resources (#238).

5. Government should:

    a. assist viable family farms threatened with bankruptcy (#242);

    b. provide more aid to family farms and less to large agricultural conglomerates (#243);

    c. reform tax policies which encourage the growth of large farms (#244);

    d. adopt research, conservation, and worker protection methods (#'s 245–247).

6. Farmworker unions should be supported (#249).

7. Urban and rural cooperation is needed to solve serious agricultural problems (#250).

D. U.S. Economy and Developing Nations

1. In our increasingly interdependent world:

    a. The preferential option for the poor focuses our attention on the Third World (#252).

    b. Developing countries perceive themselves as dependent on industrialized countries, especially the U.S. (#253).

    c. Individual nations, multinational institutions, and transnational corporations are primary actors (#255).

    d. The moral task is to work for a just international order in face of increasing interdependency (#'s 256–257).

2. Catholic social teaching emphasizes love, solidarity, justice, respect for rights, and the special place of the poor as key considerations in forming policy (#258).

3. Fundamental reform in international economic order is called for, with preferential option for the poor the central priority (#'s 259–260).
4. U.S. has central role in building just global economy:
   a. greater support of United Nations (#261);
   b. more attention to human need and less to political strategic concerns (#262);
   c. more cooperation in North-South dialogue (#263).
5. U.S. policy should promote greater social justice in developing world through key policy areas of:
   a. Development assistance: more aid, more multilateral, less military (#'s 265–266);
   b. Trade: fair prices for raw materials and better access for products, while assisting U.S. workers' adjustment needs (#'s 267–270);
   c. Finance: dealing with extremely serious debt problem in ways that do not hurt the poor (#'s 271–277);
   d. Private investment: encourage it while safeguarding against inequitable consequences (#'s 278–280).
6. World food problems offer case of special urgency:
   a. U.S. is in key position and should assist in both long-term and short-term responses (#'s 281–284);
   b. Population policies must be designed as part of overall strategies of integral human development (#'s 285–287).
7. U.S. has a special responsibility to use economic power to serve human dignity and rights, pursuing justice and peace on global scale (#'s 288–292).

IV. A New American Experiment

Preliminary Remarks
1. The founders' attempts to establish justice, the general welfare, and liberty have not been completed (#295).
2. This task calls for new forms of cooperation to create just structures and expand economic participation (#'s 296–297).

A. Cooperation within Firms and Industries
1. Workers and managers need to work together (#299).
2. Profit sharing, worker management, and worker ownership can enhance productivity and justice (#'s 300–301).
3. All sectors should accept a fair share of the sacrifices entailed in making a firm competitive (#303).

B. Local and Regional Cooperation
1. Development of new business is key to revitalizing depressed areas (#309).

    2. Entrepreneurs, government, existing business, and the local churches can work together as partners to support revitalization efforts (#'s 309–311).

C. Partnership in Development of National Policies

    1. Economy is inescapably social and political in nature (#313).

    2. Government and private groups need to work together, planning to form national policy (#'s 314–318).

    3. Impact of economic policies on the poor is "the primary criterion for judging their moral value" (#319).

    4. Massive defense spending is a "serious distortion" of economic policy (#320).

D. International Cooperation

    1. Democracy is closely tied to economic justice (#322).

    2. Existing global structures are not adequate for promoting justice (#323).

    3. U.S. should support the United Nations in alleviating poverty in developing countries (#324).

V. Commitment to the Future

A. The Christian Vocation in the World

    1. Conversion of the heart begins and accompanies structural transformation (#328).

    2. Eucharist empowers people to transform society (#330).

    3. Laity have the vocation to bring the Gospel to economic affairs (#332).

    4. Leisure should be used to build family (#338).

B. Challenges to the Church

    1. Church needs to educate the poor and all its members to social justice (#'s 340–343).

    2. Economic arrangements must promote the family (#346).

    3. Church must be exemplary as economic actor (#347):

        a. pay just wages (#352);

        b. respect the rights of its employees (#353);

        c. make responsible use of its investments and properties (#'s 354–355);

        d. promote work of charity and justice, such as Campaign for Human Development (#'s 356–357).

    4. Church commits itself to be model of collaboration and participation (#358).

C. Road Ahead

    1. Institutions and ministries of Church will continue to reflect on these important issues (#'s 360–361).

2. Universities and study groups should pursue further research into areas that need continued exploration.

D. Commitment to the Kingdom

1. We must include everyone on the globe in our dream of economic justice (#363).
2. We must move from independence through interdependence to solidarity (#365).

22

TO THE ENDS OF THE EARTH

Pastoral Statement of the United States Bishops, 1986

Major Areas of Concern
—Church as Mission
—Colonialism and Missionaries
—Total Human Liberation
—True Inculturation
—Option for the Poor
—Mission Spirituality

The pastoral states that concern for mission springs from a sense of discipleship. It notes the importance of the local church in mission sending and receiving. The statement articulates a new understanding of Church as mission and stresses that the proper focus of mission is on the physical and spiritual needs of people in the communities. The statement concludes by suggesting a spirituality for missionary activity.

HISTORICAL NOTE

The United States Bishops promulgated this statement to affirm missionaries and to stimulate a sense of personal responsibility in all Catholics for missions. The statement was heavily influenced by Vatican II's *The Missionary Activity of the Church*, Pope Paul VI's *Evangelization in the*

Modern World, and Pope John Paul II's *The Apostles to the Slavic People*. In formulating this statement the Bishops relied extensively on principles they first developed in their peace and economic letters.

Introduction

1. Jesus was a missionary (#1).
2. When we promote missionary activity, we are most faithful to the Church (#2).
3. Purpose of statement (#3):
   a. stimulate a sense of personal responsibility;
   b. affirm missionaries.
4. Essential principles for mission are found in *The Missionary Activity of the Church* and *Evangelization in the Modern World* (#4).
5. Concern for mission springs from sense of discipleship articulated in peace and economics pastorals (#6).

I. Missionary Context

A. Historical Background
1. Roots of U.S. Church are in missionary activity (#10).
2. Nineteenth and twentieth centuries: missionaries accompanied immigrants (#11).
3. U.S. Church sent and sends missionaries to other lands (#12).
4. Propagation of Faith and Holy Childhood associations have significantly aided missionaries (#13).

B. Contemporary Developments
1. A new vitality in Latin America, Africa, and Asia (#14).
2. Every local church: mission sending and receiving (#15).

C. A New Self-Understanding
1. Church equals mission (#16).
2. Basic task: spiritual and physical well-being of communities (#17).
3. Colonizing efforts brought strengths and weaknesses of Western civilization (#18).
4. U.S. missionaries: in union with local church, not U.S. government (#19).
5. Missionaries must distinguish their efforts from colonial practices (#20).

II. Today's Task

A. Theological Characteristics
1. Task is rooted in and inspired by Trinity (#22).

2. Mission's urgency springs from Jesus and looks to Kingdom (#'s 23–24).
3. Apostles were foundation of Church and Church continues Jesus' mission (#'s 25–26).
4. Mission: Church's "greatest and holiest duty" (#27).
5. Physical and spiritual needs of others demand response (#28).
6. Dangers from proselytizing are real (#29).
7. Ecumenical efforts: appropriate in prayer, media, social action (#29).

B. **Hunger for the Word**
   1. Spiritual and physical oppression create a hunger for justice and the Word (#30).
   2. People: saved as individuals and members of sociocultural groups (#31).
   3. Mission: characterized by respect and concern, not domination (#32).

C. **Mutuality in Mission**
   1. Sharing of the Gospel is essential for local churches (#'s 33, 35).
   2. We must be open to the Gospel expressed in a variety of cultures (#36).
   3. We need to link Christian values with the good in a culture (#37).
   4. Mission is not coercive (#39).

D. **Mission and Dialogue**
   1. Dialogue is necessary for extending Christ's invitation (#40).
   2. We must share with the other great religions (#41).
   3. Conversion is the goal of missions (#42).
   4. Pope John Paul II: Church can offer the "fullness of revealed truth" (#43).
   5. True inculturation: Gospel permeates culture (#44).

E. **Holistic Approach**
   1. Gospel demands response to genuine needs (#45).
   2. Jesus' mission: liberation (#46).
   3. Holy See calls for freedom from cultural, political, economic, and social slavery (#46).
   4. Jesus' mission requires our action (#'s 47–48).
   5. "The church's mission makes a special option for the poor and powerless" (#49).
   6. Evangelization of the powerful is needed (#50).

III. Mission Spirituality

1. Prayerful, Gospel-based spirituality is central to mission (#'s 51, 60).

2. Multiplication of loaves points to sharing (#53).
3. Baptism, Confirmation, and Eucharist nourish mission (#'s 52, 55, 58).
4. Discipleship requires self-denial and gift of life (#'s 56, 59).

Conclusion

1. Young people challenged to become missionaries (#61).
2. Lay missionaries are important (#63).
3. U.S. Catholics have generously supported missionary activity (#'s 64, 66).
4. Education for mission is needed by all Catholics (#70).
5. Gratitude and support for missionaries offered (#'s 72, 73).

23

THE STRUGGLE AGAINST POVERTY: A SIGN OF HOPE IN OUR WORLD

Pastoral Letter of the Canadian Episcopal Commission for Social Affairs, 1996

> **Major Areas of Concern**
> —Solidarity with the Poor
> —Women and Poverty
> —Scripture and the Poor
> —Social Sin and Redistributive Reform

The Canadian bishops focus on poverty in Canada and the world in this pastoral letter. They begin by describing characteristics of poverty, noting that it is a "complex phenomenon" that disproportionately affects women and children. The bishops contend that the eradication of poverty must be "the top priority" on the national public policy agenda. They highlight the scriptural basis for the focus on abolishing poverty and urge Christians to work against structural injustice and for genuine redistributive reform that will strengthen civil society. The bishops emphasize the need for solidarity with poor people in Canada and throughout the world.

HISTORICAL NOTE

This pastoral letter represents an important attempt by a national conference of bishops both to follow Vatican II's directive to "read the signs of the times" and to urge its audience to embrace Pope John Paul II's insistence on solidarity with the poor. The letter examines the economic situation of Canada and the world in the mid-1990s and finds an unequal sharing in prosperity, extensive poverty, and widespread economic uncertainty. The bishops emphasize job creation, trade reform, and fair taxation policies as ways to achieve solidarity and eliminate poverty.

Introduction

1. The struggle to eradicate poverty is a sign of the times and a sign of hope.
2. "God's intention [is] that the good things of the earth be shared by all humankind."

I. How to Recognize the Poor Today

1. Poverty symbolizes marginalization and exclusion.
2. Poverty is a "complex phenomenon" caused by a combination of environmental factors, private or public corruption, illness, disability, the lack of personal initiative, and the economic processes we create.
3. One out of every six Canadians lives in poverty (with the highest rate being that of single mothers).
4. Poverty "must remain the top priority on the social policy agenda."
5. "Solving the problem of poverty among women is the key to eliminating poverty in Canada."
6. For aboriginal people in Canada, the infant mortality rate is double, the unemployment rate is triple, and the income level is less than half of the Canadian population in general.
7. The poverty rate is higher for newly arriving immigrants than for people born in Canada.
8. "Escalating economic need forces both parents to work longer in order to satisfy their family's basic needs."
9. "Children in single-parent families were four times more likely to be poor than those in dual-parent households."

II. To Further the Liberating Work of God

1. Scripture reminds us "that it is God's will that our brothers and sisters be freed from oppression and from insults to their human dignity."
2. Liberation from slavery and the Covenant's concern for the poor are two hallmarks of the Old Testament's preoccupation with justice.
3. Jesus chose a life of simplicity that "illustrated the preferential option for the poor."
4. The first Christians placed "a tremendous value" on the communal sharing of goods.

III. Working for Justice

1. Christians are called to denounce "social sin that oppresses and impoverishes their brothers and sisters."
2. "Personal conversion and true repentance" can contribute to the eradication of structural injustice.
3. "The moral quality of economic growth can also be measured by how it is shared."
4. The world needs a new global ethic that results in "economic democratization, genuine redistributive reforms, and the resulting strengthening of civil society."

IV. Taking Up the Path of Solidarity

1. "The People of God must commit themselves to solidarity with the poor and their organizations in order to transform the world."
2. A pastoral methodology for solidarity includes:
   a. "being present and listening to the poor;
   b. "developing a critical analysis of the economic, political and social structures that cause poverty;
   c. "making judgments in light of Gospel principles;
   d. "stimulating creative thought and action regarding alternative visions and models for social and economic development; and
   e. "acting in solidarity with community-based movements."
3. The Church needs to have a "deep solidarity" with the new victims of global economic restructuring: fishery workers, coal miners, office workers, and others.
4. Solidarity with "Peoples of the South" will include debt for-

giveness, fair trade practices, and investment in human development such as health and education.

5. Policies that promote solidarity with fellow Canadians include fair tax reform, job creation, lowering interest rates, and the support of social programs.

6. "The fight against poverty through redistributive policies [should be] at the top of national priorities."

7. "The most effective anti-poverty remedy in Canada today is a good and steady job."

8. There is an "urgent need to adopt the preferential option for the poor."

9. "Labour movements directed toward the eradication of poverty" deserve support.

10. "We must derive continuing inspiration from the prophetic force of the witness of the Gospel, our source of hope for a better world."

24

Strangers No Longer: Together on the Journey of Hope

A Pastoral Letter Concerning Migration from the Catholic Bishops of Mexico and the United States, 2003

Major Areas of Concern
—Globalization
—Structural Injustice
—Solidarity
—Human Rights
—Legalized Immigration

Strangers No Longer begins by listing factors contributing to and injustices resulting from migration from Mexico to the United States. The document notes the common role of immigration in the history of each nation as well as the faith in Jesus Christ that many citizens of the two nations share. The pastoral letter then enumerates five principles of Catholic social teaching that guide the bishops' views on migration issues. *Strangers No Longer* concludes with a discussion of the pastoral and public policy challenges Mexico and the United States face concerning migration.

HISTORICAL NOTE

Strangers No Longer is the result of a two-year collaborative process of the bishops of Mexico and the United States. The process, as well as much of the substance of the document itself, was inspired by Pope John Paul II's 1999 apostolic exhortation, *Ecclesia in America,* which resulted from the Synod of Bishops of America. *Strangers No Longer* notes with gratitude the dialogue begun by the presidents of Mexico and the United States concerning migration issues and seeks to influence public policies the bishops hope will stem from these meetings.

Introduction

1. Increased migration in the Americas resulting from globalization is a sign of the times (#1).
2. The bishops of both countries agree this migration is beneficial, but are concerned with the suffering, dying, human rights abuses, separation of families, and racist attitudes that now accompany it (#2).
3. Christ is present in migrants. They and all who deal with them are vulnerable because our social structures do not meet their basic needs (#'s 3–5).
4. We are to be judged by how we treat the most vulnerable. We seek a more just legal system in line with Catholic social teaching that supports migration, welcoming strangers among us (#'s 6–7).
5. We appreciate and encourage every sign of commitment to solidarity as we speak now to migrants, public officials, government personnel, and the peoples of the United States and Mexico of the singular opportunity we have to develop a more just, generous system of immigration (#'s 8–12).

I. America: A Common History of Migration and a Shared Faith in Jesus Christ

1. Mexico and America are both countries of immigrants, conquerors, colonizers, refugees, exiles, and persecuted who came to form new civilizations, bringing energy, diversity, and hope (#'s 13–17).
2. The interdependence and integration of the United States and Mexico are evident in large migration flows, investment flows,

and, especially, the Christian spiritual connections that demand just and loving relationships among the diverse peoples, rejecting discrimination and violence (#'s 18–20).

II. Reflections in the Light of the Word of God and Catholic Social Teaching

1. The Word of God and Catholic social teaching offer a hopeful understanding of the social, cultural, economic, political, and ethical aspects of migration and its causes (#22).

2. God liberated the Israelites from Egyptian slavery and accompanied their migration. They learned to care for migrants and refugees as God cared for them (#25).

3. Christian migrants and refugees can draw strength from the fact that Jesus, Mary, and Joseph were refugees fleeing to Egypt and from Jesus' identification with the stranger in the parable of the Last Judgment (#26).

4. The Holy Spirit works throughout history against injustice, division, and oppression and for human rights and racial and cultural solidarity (#27).

5. Catholic social teaching recognizes the right to migrate and demands that poverty, injustice, religious intolerance, and armed conflict—the root causes of migration—be addressed. Pope Pius XII insisted that everyone has "the right to conditions worthy of human life" and the right to migrate when these are not available (#'s 28–29).

6. States have the right to control their borders, but it is not an absolute right and must be measured against the needs of migrants and refugees. Stronger states have a greater obligation to serve the universal common good by taking in migrants and refugees (#'s 30–31).

7. Stemming underdevelopment throughout the world will help stem illegal immigration. Migrants' rights and dignity are to be respected whether they are legal or not (#32).

8. Five principles of Catholic social teaching that guide the Church's view on migration issues are:
   a. Economic opportunities must be available in one's own country (#34).
   b. The goods of the earth belong to everyone, so people have the right to migrate when their countries of origin cannot provide those opportunities (#35).
   c. States have the right to control borders but should accommodate migration (#36).
   d. Refugees from persecution and wars have a right to be received without the threat of prison (#37).

     e. Human dignity and human rights must be respected no matter what the person's legal status (#38).

9. Violations of human rights, including the right to migrate, are a violation of the common good. In today's world of poverty and persecution, the presumption is that people must migrate (#39).

III. Pastoral Challenges and Responses

1. Seeing Christ in migrants brings about conversion to communion and solidarity with them. This involves overcoming forms of cultural superiority and discovering their values and faith traditions (#40).
2. Catholic communities everywhere should offer welcome and belonging (#41).
3. Bishops should build that spirit of hospitality in their communities with all the services it entails. Church leaders and communities must seek justice for migrants and systemic change to protect their rights (#'s 42–43).
4. Migrant families should have access to social service networks, legal and medical aid, and pastoral counseling (#'s 44–45).
5. Migrants can be evangelizers by the way they live. They need to have the sacraments made available to them. The families that migrants leave behind also need special pastoral care (#'s 46–47).
6. The Bishops' Conferences in Mexico and the United States should cooperate to foster various types of ministry to migrants and immigrants. They should offer preparation that includes language, intercultural training, and spirituality to those entering this ministry and provide training in pastoral migration as part of all seminary and ministry curricula. They should encourage dialogue, exchanges, and high level episcopal collaboration (#'s 48–54).

IV. Public Policy Challenge and Responses

1. Current Mexican and U.S. migration policies are inconsistent. They should be reformed and coordinated to respect migrants' dignity, recognize the needs for migration resulting from globalization, and "create a generous, legal flow of migrants." Our policy proposals address root causes of and legal avenues for migration, as well as humane law enforcement (#'s 56–58).
2. A weak economy in Mexico forces people to migrate. Economic policies such as the North American Free Trade Agreement (NAFTA) have harmed small businesses and should therefore be reconsidered. Economic inequality between nations must be overcome (#60).

3. Mexican public policy should favor the creation of low-skilled living-wage jobs and the rebuilding of the agricultural and small business sectors, especially in areas with the highest emigration rates and in border areas (#'s 61–62).

4. U.S. visa limits divide families and encourage undocumented migration by family members. This must be changed and special attention given to protecting the rights of the children of migrants (#'s 63–67).

5. The large numbers of undocumented migrants are quietly accepted because they are useful to business and government. Legalizing them would stabilize labor markets, unify families, improve living standards for immigrants, maintain the flow of remittances to Mexico, guarantee safe passage, protect basic labor rights, and enable more accurate population statistics (#'s 68–71).

6. The United States needs Mexican laborers and should provide permanent and temporary visa programs for laborers, protect their rights, and guarantee a living family wage, social security, and benefits. The United States should sign the International Convention on the Protection of the Rights of All Migrant Workers and Members of their Families, and Mexico should drop its reservations (#'s 72–77).

7. Border patrols and government migration authorities must reform their enforcement policies and tactics, respect the human dignity of migrants, and avoid violence. Migrants are not criminals and must not be treated as such (#'s 78–80).

8. Mexican minors must be treated with respect for their age. Current treatment is shameful (#82).

9. Mexican authorities must stop violence against migrants and corruption in the migration system. Both the United States and Mexico must train agents in enforcement tactics that protect human rights (#'s 83–85).

10. U.S. and Mexican border blockade initiatives have driven migrants to life-endangering border crossing areas and into the hands of smugglers. These tactics must be stopped and smuggling must be ended (#'s 86–89).

11. Both countries must work to end trafficking in persons (#'s 90–91).

12. In the United States, the Illegal Immigration Reform and Immigrant Responsibility Act of 1996 must be corrected to protect due process and prevent the unjust separation of families. The Mexican government too must honor the right of all migrants to due process. Captured migrants should have access to social services and not be treated as criminals (#'s 92–94).

13. Asylum seekers and refugees entering both countries are being turned away without appropriate screening and protections. They should have access to qualified legal authorities. A regional process should be developed with Central American countries (#99).

14. The September 11 terrorist attacks demand greater security against future threats, but must not be allowed to cut back migration or refugee flows or reduce human rights protections (#100).

Conclusion

1. Migration is an authentic "sign of the times" calling us to transform social structures so that they serve the development of all and promote solidarity (#'s 101–102).

2. The Church is called to be a sign and instrument of the unity of all people and should provide welcome, joy, charity, and hope to everyone, especially to those suffering poverty, marginalization, and exclusion (#103).

3. We ask public leaders and media in both countries to achieve a more generous, just, and humane system of migration (#104).

4. We commit ourselves to welcome and defend migrants—not as strangers but as sisters and brothers in God—and to work for the conditions that enable them to thrive in their own homeland if they wish. May they find hope and share their faith and cultural values as treasures wherever they go (#'s 105–108).

25

THE MEDELLÍN CONFERENCE DOCUMENTS

Second Meeting of the Latin American Episcopal Conference, 1968

Major Areas of Concern
—Structural Justice
—Liberation
—Participation
—Marxism and Capitalism
—Political Reform
—Conscientization
—Arms Race
—Violence

The Latin American Bishops—meeting at Medellín, Colombia, in 1968—issued a number of documents on the life of the Latin American church. The documents on justice and peace (outlined here) apply Catholic social teaching to the Latin American situation. The documents state the need for just structures that promote liberation and participation. Political reform, individual and communal conscientization, and an end to violence are necessary conditions for justice and peace in Latin America.

HISTORICAL NOTE

The second meeting of the Latin American Episcopal Conference—held at Medellín, Colombia, in 1968—coincided with Pope Paul VI's visit to Bogota. Influenced by Vatican II, the social teachings of John XXIII and Paul VI, liberation theology, and the reality of life in Latin America, the Bishops made a seminal and fundamental criticism of society and a strong commitment to the poor.

JUSTICE

I. Pertinent Facts

1. Misery expresses itself as injustice (#1).
2. Recent efforts have not insured justice (#1).
3. Universal frustration of legitimate aspirations exists (#1).
4. Lack of social-cultural integration has caused unjust economic and political structures (#2).

II. Doctrinal Bases

1. God creates people and gives them power to transform and perfect the world (#3).
2. Jesus: liberator from sin, hunger, oppression, misery, ignorance (#3).
3. Authentic liberation requires personal and structural transformation (#3).
4. Divine work equals integral human development and liberation (#4).
5. Love is Christian dynamism (#4).
6. Dignity of human person results in unity of society (#5).
7. Justice: demand of biblical teaching (#5).

III. Projections for Social-Pastoral Planning

A. Direction of Social Change
1. Structures should ensure that all, especially lower classes, participate in society (#7).
2. Families: natural unit of society, should organize so needs can be met (#8).
3. Professional organizations and peasants: organize to demand human and dignified work (#9).

    4. Both Marxism and capitalism "militate against the dignity of the human person" (#10).

    5. Many workers experience physical, cultural, and spiritual slavery (#11).

    6. Participation is necessary for just economic system (#11).

    7. Unions "should acquire sufficient strength and power" (#12).

    8. Socialization: necessary for unity, liberation, development (#13).

    9. Rural transformation needed (#14):

       a. "human promotion of peasants and Indians";

       b. reform of agrarian structures and policies.

    10. Industrialization: necessary process for development (#15).

B. Political Reform

    1. Purpose of political authority is common good (#16).

    2. Political reform needs to address structural change (#16).

    3. Political authority: duty to promote participation (#16).

C. Information and Conscientization

    1. Formation of social conscience is indispensable (#17).

    2. People in decision-making positions deserve special attention (#19).

    3. Small, basic communities are essential for this task (#20).

    4. Mass media should be used for human promotion (#23).

PEACE

I. Latin American Situation

A. Class Tensions

    1. Different forms of marginality: socio-economic, cultural, racial, religious, etc. (#2).

    2. Extreme social inequality exists; majority has very little (#3).

    3. Inequality breeds frustration and low morale (#4).

    4. Privileged are insensitive to misery of marginalized (#5).

    5. Dominant class uses power unjustly (#6).

    6. The oppressed are increasingly aware of their situation (#7).

B. International Tension

    1. Most Latin American countries depend on an external economic power (#8).

    2. International commerce is distorted economically (#9).

    3. Economic and human capital is invested excessively in foreign countries (#9).

    4. A progressive international debt hinders development (#9).

    5. International imperialism creates conditions of dependency (#9).

C. Tensions within Latin America

    1. Exacerbated nationalism contributes to tensions (#12).

    2. The arms race is beyond reason (#13).

II. Doctrinal Reflections

A. Christian View of Peace
1. Peace is a work of justice (#14).
2. Peace is a permanent task (#14).
3. Peace is the result of love (#14).

B. Violence
1. Violence is one of Latin America's greatest problems (#15).
2. Structural justice is a prerequisite for peace (#15).
3. Temptation to violence is strong (#16).
4. Wealthy and fearful must work together for peace (#'s 17–18).
5. People should not put their hopes in violence (#19).

III. Pastoral Conclusions

1. To form the consciences of Latin Americans to peace, justice, and the rights of the poor (#'s 21–22).
2. To encourage Catholic institutions to foster vocations of service (#25).
3. To urge an end to arms race, violence, and domination (#'s 29, 32).

26

THE PUEBLA CONFERENCE DOCUMENT

Third Meeting of the Latin American Episcopal Conference, 1979

Major Areas of Concern
—Evangelization
—Human Dignity
—Liberation
—Base Communities
—Role of the Laity
—Option for the Poor

The Latin American Episcopal Conference—meeting at Puebla, Mexico, in 1979—issued a document that confirmed its statements at Medellín (1968) and placed the entire mission of the Church in the context of evangelization. The document begins by examining the problems confronting the people of Latin America and the role of the Church in solving these problems. The Bishops then consider God's plan for human beings and the ways that liberation and evangelization can cooperate with this plan. The Bishops next emphasize the roles of base communities and the laity in helping the Church carry out its mission. The Bishops conclude with a strong affirmation of the option for the poor and the option for young people.

HISTORICAL NOTE

The third meeting of the Latin American Bishops, coinciding with Pope John Paul II's journey to Mexico, confirmed Medellín's mandate that the Church evangelize for the poor, for liberation, and for an end to unjust social structures. Although many of the leading progressive Bishops of Latin America were not appointed delegates and most of the region's prominent liberation theologians were not chosen as experts, the conference's final document supported the basic thrust of the social significance of the Church's mission to the world.

I. Pastoral Overview of Latin America

A. Problems

1. Loneliness, family problems, and lack of meaning plague many people (#27).
2. The poverty of millions of peasants, indigenous, and young people is devastating and humiliating (#'s 29, 32–35).
3. Abuse of power has resulted in repression and violation of human rights (#'s 41–42).
4. Materialism has subverted public and private values (#55).
5. Economic, cultural, political, and technological dependence neglects human dignity (#'s 64–66).

B. The Church

1. Present church structures do not meet people's need for the Gospel (#78).
2. Indifferentism, not atheism, is a major problem among intellectuals and professionals (#79).
3. The people are demanding justice, freedom, and respect for rights (#87).
4. Marxism, capitalism, and political activity of priests present dilemmas for the Church (#92).
5. Church supports the people's yearning for a "full and integral liberation" (#141).
6. New social structures and the role of the laity need to be emphasized for Church to fulfill its mission (#'s 152–154).

II. God's Saving Plan

A. Jesus

1. The person of Jesus must not be distorted, factionalized, or ideologized (#178).
2. Jesus "rejects the temptation of political power and the temptation to violence" (#192).

  3. Jesus calls for a radical discipleship and a love that give a privileged place to the poor (#'s 192–193).
  4. Jesus has planted the Kingdom and justice of God in human history (#197).

B. Human Beings
  1. Determinism, psychologism, economism, statism, and scientism offer only partial vision of the human being (#'s 307–315).
  2. Church proclaims the "inviolable nobility" and dignity of each human being (#317).
  3. Freedom is the gift and task of human beings (#321).
  4. Human dignity is rooted in God and renewed in Jesus (#'s 327–330).

C. Evangelization
  1. Evangelization "aims at personal conversion and social transformation" (#362).
  2. Evangelization seeks to get at the core of a culture to bring about conversion (#388).
  3. Urban-industrial culture, accompanied by personalization and socialization, challenges evangelization (#416).
  4. Secularism "separates human beings from God" (#435).
  5. The people's religiosity is both a way the people evangelize themselves and an object of evangelization (#450).

D. Liberation
  1. Catholic social teaching indicates that the entire Christian community is responsible for evangelization and liberation (#474).
  2. Liberation is enacted on the truth about: Jesus, the Church, and human beings (#484).
  3. Liberation does not use violence or the dialectics of class struggle (#486).
  4. Equality of all peoples, freedom, justice, and self-determination are legitimate aspirations of the people (#'s 502–504).

III. Evangelization

A. Base Communities
  1. Base communities foster interrelationships, acceptance of God's word, and reflection on reality and the Gospel (#629).
  2. Base communities bring families together in intimate relationships grounded in faith (#641).
  3. Base communities embody the Church's preferential love for the common people (#644).

B. Role of the Laity
  1. There is a growing need for the presence of lay people in evangelization (#777).

2. An atmosphere of maturity and realism now exists and will promote dialogue and participation in the Church (#781).
3. A clerical mentality and a divorce between faith and life hinder participation in the Church (#'s 783–784).
4. The family, education, social communications, and political activity require the special attention of the laity (#'s 790–791).
5. Lay people need "to acquire a solid overall human formation" to participate more effectively in the mission of the Church (#794).
6. Women have been pushed to the margins of society (#834).
7. Women possess full equality and dignity, and have a significant role to play in the mission of the Church (#'s 841, 845).

IV. A Missionary Church

A. Option for the Poor
1. The poor have been encouraged by the Church (#1137).
2. Jesus' mission is directed to, at first, the poor (#1143).
3. The poor challenge the Church to conversion, service, and solidarity (#1147).
4. Option for the poor requires changes in unjust political, economic, and social structures (#1155).
5. Conversion to evangelize and eliminate poverty demands "an austere lifestyle and a total confidence in the Lord" (#1158).

B. Option for Young People
1. Young people represent "an enormous force for renewal" (#1178).
2. Young people should experience the Church as "a place of communion and participation" (#1184).
3. Church wants to help young people become factors of change (#1187).
4. Church hopes to introduce young people to the living Christ (#1194).

27

TO THE PEOPLE OF GOD JOURNEYING IN CENTRAL AMERICA

Pastoral Letter of the Bishops of Central America, 2002

Major Areas of Concern
—Poverty
—Debt
—Human Rights
—Migration
—Development
—Mission

To the People of God Journeying in Central America opens by listing factors that "disrupt and threaten peace," including unemployment, migration, debt and the growing gap between the rich and the poor. The pastoral letter then details several problems associated with migration and the "endless human rights abuses" that the region has experienced. The bishops give voice to several characteristics of just development, including food security and respect for "human ecology." The letter ends with the bishops stating their commitment to a regional "Missionary Year" that will be marked by "solidarity and fraternity."

HISTORICAL NOTE

The bishops of Central America issued *To the People of God Journeying in Central America* at the conclusion of their annual meeting in 2002. The bishops were especially mindful of possible threats and opportunities associated with the Central America Free Trade Agreement and the Free Trade Area of the Americas, and used the opportunity to reflect on fair and just development. As part of their meeting, the bishops hosted a delegation of bishops and lay Catholics from the United States and engaged in joint discussion on the issue of migration from Central America to the United States and South America. The bishops also use the pastoral letter to launch a region-wide "Missionary Year," designed to enlarge the focus of their churches.

A. **Challenges Facing the Churches and Societies**
   1. Factors that "disrupt and threaten peace" include "growing unemployment, migration, the increase in external and internal debt, the growing gap between the rich and the poor, the lack of credibility among public institutions," and other problems (#1).
   2. Poverty forces many Central Americans "to leave their homes to seek better living conditions abroad" (#2).
   3. Negative aspects of this migration include: "cultural uprooting, frequent and humiliating deportations, and fragmentation of the family of origin" (#2).
   4. The positive effect of migration is the increase in "families' income in the migrants' home countries" (#2).
   5. "We have also verified endless human rights abuses, which seem to have no solution and which give us a sense of weakness in the face of the disproportionate strength of the powers of this world" (#2).
   6. "Migration from El Salvador, Guatemala, and Honduras is aimed at the North, migration from Nicaragua is increasingly directed toward the South" (#3).
   7. "We see increasing deterioration of values, particularly the value of the family" (#3).
   8. There is "an increase in corruption in the public and private sphere which results in public distrust" (#3).
   9. "Our people live in insecurity and fear" (#3).
   10. The bishops are not opposed "in principle" to a free trade agreement but do not want it to "jeopardize the interest of citizens, especially in our case, of peasant farmers" (#4).
   11. Development must:
       a. be "equitable and sustainable;"

     b. "ensure food security;"

     c. "protect small and medium-size businesses;" and

     d. "respect 'human ecology' which is rooted in the family" (#4).

B. A New Commitment

1. "We greet with gratitude and satisfaction the renewed commitment of our lay people who show themselves to be increasingly dedicated to the process of the New Evangelization" (#3).

2. The bishops open a region-wide "Missionary Year" because "mission is the very identity of the Church" (#5).

3. "We see an urgent need to move from a ministry that is concerned with caretaking and preserving what our Churches have achieved so far toward a ministry marked by a commitment to mission and evangelization" (#5).

4. The bishops make a "commitment to a more Christian Central America marked by solidarity and fraternity" (#6).

28

ETHICAL AND GOSPEL IMPERATIVES FOR OVERCOMING DIRE POVERTY AND HUNGER

National Conference of the Bishops of Brazil, 2002

Major Areas of Concern
—Hunger
—Increasing Inequality
—Reasons for Hunger
—Use of Land and Natural Resources
—Change of Attitude

The National Conference of Bishops of Brazil (CNBB) issued this statement on hunger in April 2002. They stress that food should not be treated as another commodity; human beings have a right to sufficient and suitable food.

HISTORICAL NOTE

This statement, one of many on social issues, came from the meeting of the Brazilian bishops conference in April 2002. Besides the teaching, the bishops called for a mobilization of volunteers to tackle specific projects and campaigns. In January 2003, the new government under President Lula (Luis Inacio da Silva) announced a major campaign to eliminate hunger.

Introduction

In taking on the joys and hopes, anxieties and sorrows of the Brazilian people, we are scandalized by the fact that there is enough food for everyone, but hunger is prevalent, and due to bad distribution of property and income (#'s 1–4).

I. Pressing Challenges at the End of the Millennium

1. The twentieth century leaves a legacy of war and genocide, leaving millions of victims. Social inequality is increasing as the result of the globalization of the market, which concentrates power and wealth, while diminishing employment, degrading nature, and excluding people (#6).
2. We also inherit progress and science in technology. We have the resources and technology to overcome hunger. What is missing is the gospel spirit of solidarity to give up privileges and free us from the virus of selfishness. Political will is also missing (#9).

A. Drama of Hunger in Brazil

1. Although some say that there is not enough food for everyone, the root of the problem of hunger lies in the iniquitous distribution of income and wealth (#11).
2. The market rewards the strong and punishes the weak, increases unemployment and pays workers very little (#13).
3. Other problems include the weakening of the state's regulatory role, high bank interest rates, and rising unemployment (#14).
4. The evil of the system is that it gives priority to the market, and profit, and to finance capital rather than recognizing and promoting first the dignity of the person and access of the poor to worthy conditions of food, work, housing, health education, and leisure (#15).
5. The media foster the idea that "money brings happiness" even as they trample Christian values (#16).

B. Basic Issue: Change of Attitude

1. The contrast between the dire poverty of people in slums and tenements, who are pushed even to drug trafficking and prostitution to survive, and the luxury and sophistication of gated condominiums is unacceptable (#18).
2. Social justice is an offense against God, who created us in his image and likeness. Rescuing the dignity of the poor should be

more than emergency help; the society and economy must be changed into a new order aimed at the common good (#20).

3. Are we willing to recognize our attachment to material things? How can we bring about solidarity in the church, like the first Christian communities? (#21).

4. The CNBB invites all to personal and community conversion away from selfishness and consumerism to overcoming dire poverty (#22).

II. Gospel Demands

1. Food is gift of God the creator to all creatures without exception (#23).

2. The people of Israel show that overcoming hunger is intrinsic to faith. The prophets show the connection between worship and the practice of justice (human rights of the oppressed) (#24).

3. Sharing another's suffering like Jesus is not giving things, but giving one's self (#26).

4. Compassion means being in solidarity, spending time and resources organizing the poor—not *doing for* the poor but *doing with* them. Liberation entails a group process; no one is liberated alone (#32).

III. Ethical Demands

1. No one should be in danger of falling into dire poverty or going hungry. *Food security* entails quantity and quality of food, in an ongoing way, suited to one's culture. Food must not be treated as just another commodity. When people are going hungry it is immoral to store food for speculative profits. Just intervention and regulation by the state is in order (#35).

2. Family meals are a good time for consolidating social bonds. *Table fellowship,* which has religious value, made explicit in grace and blessing, should be encouraged (#37).

3. Food security extends to all humankind including coming generations (#38).

4. All human beings should be assured access to the *sources of life*. Land, water, air, seeds and technology should be regulated by the state, and cannot be at the mercy of private property or the market (e.g., patent laws). We urge land reform; we condemn turning water into a business; we urge a public policy of making seeds and technology available and against monopolizing of patents in the area of food (#39).

5. The universal right to food security (Article 25 of the Universal

Declaration of Human Rights) is supported by the church's social doctrine (#40).

6. Simplicity and frugality are today a condition for the survival of the human species. The current consumption pattern of the privileged cannot be extended to all. We must give up the consumerist dream, instilled by advertising, and implement a globalization in solidarity, based on a gospel-inspired way of life (#44).

7. We must reject the *sovereignty of the market* which encourages only production in view of profit. The market is a means at the service of human needs and hence must be monitored by society (#45).

8. *Financial speculation* which applies capital to futures markets negotiating merely virtual commodities rather than applying it in producing real goods, must be controlled (#46).

IV. Promotion of Social Rights

1. The 1988 constitution is innovative because it speaks of overcoming poverty and reducing social and regional inequalities, and recognizes social rights, e.g., social security, education, culture and sports, environment, etc. (#48).

2. Classic situations of vulnerability—illness, old age, widowhood, disability, unemployment, work accident—are recognized as social rights independently of employment (#49).

3. There is likewise a timid recognition of land reform (#50).

4. We have a long way to go, especially since the government emphasizes financial policy over the development of the citizenry. Social rights are recognized but little implemented (#51).

5. The promotion of the right to food and nutrition is the primary duty of the state and governments, not allowing any person to fail to have food in sufficient quality and quantity (#52).

V. Make Food, God's Gift, a Right of All

1. We call for a National Volunteer Work Campaign to overcome Dire Poverty and Hunger. A bishops commission should coordinate it nationally and regionally. We extend this to other churches and religious traditions and other organizations in Brazilian society (#57).

2. In the diocese people should be invited to form groups (#58).

3. Such National Work Project groups should identify needs of the municipality; produce educational materials; list communi-

cations teams, prepare radio and TV spot ads, coops, propose legislation, data banks; do an evaluation (#'s 60–61).

4. This is part of the evangelization action of the church (#62).
5. Projects: campaign to build a million wells in semi-arid Northeast Brazil; Forum, national campaign to limit agricultural property; campaign to pass legislation for indigenous peoples; create committees against electoral corruption. Organize defense of national sovereignty and food security under threat from hemispheric and international treaties (#63).
6. Organize symposium for policy guidelines (#64).

VI. Conclusion "Give them to eat yourselves"

1. One of the primary signs of real evangelization at the beginning of the millennium will be the elimination of hunger caused by dire poverty in our country (#66).
2. To overcome such a huge challenge in association with people of good faith in the Catholic Church, other Christian churches and religious groups, popular movements, labor unions, government institutions, we beg God's blessing and Mary's protection (#67).

29

JUSTICE AND EVANGELIZATION IN AFRICA

Statement of the Symposium of Episcopal Conferences of Africa and Madagascar (SECAM), 1981

Major Areas of Concern
—Christian Vision of Justice
—African Reality
—Church: A Witness for Justice
—Education for Justice
—National and International Action

In 1981 the Bishops of SECAM published an exhortation on *Justice and Evangelization in Africa*. This document states the Christian vision of a just world and contrasts this vision with the situation in Africa. The Bishops issue a call for love and commitment and outline a program of pastoral response for local churches as well as a plan of action on the national and international levels.

HISTORICAL NOTE

This document is the natural cumulation of several SECAM statements on justice, especially denouncements of specific unjust situations. This exhortation is a revision of a Meetings for African Collaboration (MAC) interim report and is the product of extensive consultation between Bishops and other religious leaders.

I. Christian Vision and Today's Reality

A. Christian Vision

1. Jesus came to establish a Kingdom of life, truth, love, and justice (#3).
2. A Church is not fully rooted among its people if it does not try to establish justice (#3).
3. Old Testament (#4):
   a. God's saving justice;
   b. challenge of the prophets to the entire society to be just.
4. New Testament (#5):
   a. Christians should find in the Gospels support for justice activities;
   b. Jesus made himself the champion of the poor, oppressed, marginalized;
   c. call for justice is directed to Jesus.
5. Tradition: justice is an essential basis for Christian life (#'s 5–6).
6. Dedication to the interior virtues of justice and kindness and to the common good is needed to establish a political, social, and economic life that is truly human (#8).

B. Today's Reality in Africa

1. External factors (#'s 9–10):
   a. "liberating" foreign armed intervention creating new states of dependency;
   b. unjust distribution of resources;
   c. dialogue of deaf between North and South;
   d. hold of multinationals;
   e. pillage of raw materials from Third World;
   f. national debts.
2. Internal factors (#11):
   a. violations of human rights;
   b. dictatorships, totalitarianism, oppression;
   c. corruption of every kind.

C. **Call to Love and Commitment**
1. Only through love can Christians work in this damaged world (#13).
2. Christians need to work, educate, and commend rather than complain, criticize, and condemn (#13).

II. Pastoral Program for Local Churches

A. **Justice in the Church's Life**
1. Ongoing conversion in lifestyle and pastoral action (#15).
2. Human relationships of mutual respect (#16).
3. Financial autonomy and sobriety in lifestyle (#17).
4. Respect for cultures (#18).

B. **Education for Justice**
1. Goals (#20):
   a. understand and transmit the good news of human liberation;
   b. respect the rights of all.
2. The family: first school of justice; social and cultural changes shake its structures (#21).
3. Youth: justice and service encouraged in formation (#22).
4. Christian communities: responsible for justice in Africa through witness and action (#23).
5. Catholic Action Movements: stress the role of the laity (#24).
6. Communications: great potential for influencing public opinion (#25).

III. National and International Action

A. **National Level—Requires the participation of all**
1. Participation in life of society (#27):
   a. application of ethical principles to a society is difficult and delicate;
   b. African tradition emphasizes social responsibility as a duty;
   c. Christians should participate in public life.
2. Identification of the forms of oppression and reflection in common on this oppression, from grassroots up (#28).
3. Joint reflection and action by apostolic workers; "prophets" should speak through the Church (#29).
4. Speaking out for justice (#30):
   a. Jesus loves people and is concerned especially about the poorest and weakest;
   b. prayer for justice is essential;
   c. support of sister-churches is of great help;

      d. action for justice must be action for evangelization;

      e. first priority is to try to dialogue with those responsible for injustices.

  5. Structures need to be set up by the Church to document instances of injustices and prepare interventions for justice (#31).

B. International Level

  1. Different cultures should be respected (#32).

  2. Current international structures operate to detriment of developing countries: e.g., price of raw materials, arms race (#32).

  3. Of dramatic urgency is the problem of refugees, the number one plague of African continent (#33).

IV. Conclusion

  1. The Spirit will enable people to witness, educate, and work for justice (#34).

  2. An appeal is made to churches in the West, to understand and support African Church's efforts (#34).

30

THE FUTURE IS OURS

Pastoral Letter by the Catholic Bishops of Zambia, 1992

Major Areas of Concern
—Political Participation
—Socio-Economic Issues
—Women and Development
—Debt
—Environment

The Future Is Ours begins by commending and celebrating the 1991 "free and fair elections" in Zambia. The pastoral then notes a number of serious economic needs facing the country and outlines the responsibilities of citizens in collaborating with the new government to respond effectively to these needs. The bishops state that the Church should model accountability and openness for the government and society. The letter next suggests several national economic priorities, including the recovery of the country's agricultural potential and the forgiveness and reduction of its debt. The letter concludes by pledging respect for freedom of religion and urging Church members to put their faith into practice.

HISTORICAL NOTE

The Future Is Ours was issued in March 1992, shortly after the Chiluba government came to power and the new president began his administration by declaring Zambia a "Christian nation." The bishops were intent on taking the opportunity presented by the new government to celebrate the successful elections and call the nation and Church members to a new spirit of responsibility and participation. The document addresses themes given voice by Pope John Paul II during his 1989 visit to Zambia and further articulated in his 1991 encyclical letter, *Centesimus Annus*.

A. Introduction
  1. "As Zambia enters into the Third Republic," the Catholic bishops "have asked many of our Christian sisters and brothers to tell us of their hopes and fears, their expectations and desires" (#2).
  2. The bishops "congratulate the people of Zambia for their mature participation in free and fair elections" (#5).

B. A New Culture
  1. The bishops call for "a new moral culture of responsibility and a new political and economic culture of accountability" (#8).
  2. There is serious socio-economic need in Zambia:
      a. nearly 60 percent of households lack adequate nutrition;
      b. national output continues to decline and unemployment continues to grow;
      c. inflation has been more than 100 percent for the past several years;
      d. the country's health and education systems have almost collapsed; and
      e. AIDS is affecting "more and more families" (#9).
  3. The bishops call the people "to return to a spirit of hard work and cooperation" (#12).
  4. "The future of Zambia is primarily in our hands. . . . We must create greater self-reliance and less dependence on government and on charitable handouts" (#13).
  5. "Greater respect should be promoted for public properties and institutions" (#14).
  6. "We need to eliminate the anti-social behavior which tears apart the fabric of our communities (e.g., stealing, killing, drunkenness . . . and witchcraft)" (#15).

C. Church as Model
  1. "The Church itself should be a model for society" (#16).
  2. "We pledge to take steps toward greater openness and honesty about the decisions, actions and finances of our Church" (#16).
  3. "We will make our own efforts to involve more women in the development of our Church and Nation" (#17).
  4. "We emphasize again the urgency of dealing more effectively with the crisis of AIDS. There is need for openness about this sickness, its causes and prevention, and its consequences" (#19).

D. Democracy and Rights

1. "Central to the new political culture must be promotion of a spirit of service and accountability with the Government" (#20).
2. "The Church will monitor the activities of our Government to assure that both the political and economic rights of all are respected" (#22).
3. "In dealing with national issues, the media should be particularly sensitive to what affects the poor and powerless in our society" (#23).

E. Economics and Priorities

1. "The fundamental norm for judging the success of any economic reforms: they must serve all the people" (#25).
2. "The mechanisms of the free market must always be subject to social control to assure more equitable distribution and more effective protection of all the various goods of society" (#27).
3. "The recovery of Zambia's agricultural potential has to be the number one priority in addressing our problems" (#29).
4. "The protection of the environment must be a serious concern for our economic well-being" (#31).
5. New investments "should be the kind which generate jobs" (#32).
6. "The tax structure should assure that people with lower incomes are not forced to pay a disproportionate amount of taxes" (#34).
7. Some of "Zambia's huge external debt is . . . due to our own poor planning, inefficient management, corruption, and lack of commitment to the national welfare" (#36).
8. "The major bulk of [the debt] is due to factors simply beyond our control" including failing commodity prices, rising import prices, and increasing external interest rates (#36).
9. The bishops "join with the appeal of many Church leaders around the world in demanding large-scale forgiveness of debts" (#37).

F. Conclusion

1. "We call upon all Zambians to respect the constitutional guarantee of freedom of conscience and freedom of worship and expression" (#39).
2. "A Nation is not Christian by declaration but by deeds" (#40).
3. "We want to remind all members of our Church of the obligation to put their faith into practice" (#41).
4. "We know that the future of Zambia is not for the winning political party but for the people, all of the people" (#46).

31

ECONOMIC JUSTICE IN SOUTH AFRICA

A Pastoral Statement of the Southern African Catholic Bishops' Conference, 1999

Major Areas of Concern
—Human Dignity
—Economic Structures
—Solidarity
—Option for the Poor
—Globalization
—Role of Women
—International Trade

Economic Justice in South Africa begins by linking social problems to "basic economic injustices." The document then states the Church's prophetic duty to spread the values of the Gospel and to assist those who are perpetuating economic injustice to "see the harm they are causing." The document lists and explains a number of factors that contribute to economic injustice including poverty, unemployment, materialism, threats to family life, and environmental degradation. *Economic Justice in South Africa* next describes a number of "Christian Economic Values" including solidarity, option for the poor, and subsidiarity and applies these values to the South African and world economic situations. The document concludes with a substantial chapter on what can be done by government, business, and other key stakeholders to move the South African economy into conformity with principles of justice.

HISTORICAL NOTE

Economic Justice in South Africa was issued by the Catholic Bishops of South Africa in 1999, shortly before the nation's second democratic election. The document is the bishops' third major pastoral statement on social issues since the transition from apartheid. *A Call to Build a New South Africa* (1992) and *Free at Last* (1994) are the first two. The document acknowledges that "massive, and overwhelmingly positive political change has occurred" with the end of apartheid "but the same has not happened in the economy." The bishops operate squarely within the tradition of Catholic social teaching, describing the key principles in the doctrine and then applying them to the national economic situation.

A. Introduction
1. Many social problems are exacerbated by "basic economic injustices."
2. "In South Africa and in the world as a whole, we are sitting on an economic time-bomb."
3. "The key to achieving economic justice lies in human attitudes."

B. The Church's Prophetic Duty
1. The Church has "a sacred duty to preach the Good News and to spread the values of the Gospel."
2. The Church assists the victims of injustice and acts "also in order to bring those responsible for unjust systems and practices to see the harm they are causing."

C. Discerning Economic Justice
1. "At the heart of every economic system lie human needs, human abilities and human decisions."
2. The choices which humans make "determine the justice or injustice of the economic system."
3. Every economy has a moral quality "that enables us to make judgments about whether or not it is a just economy."
4. Factors that contribute to the injustice of an economy include:
   a. poverty;
   b. unemployment;
   c. inequitable distribution of resources;
   d. discrimination against women;
   e. materialism;

     f. greed;

     g. threats to family life; and

     h. environmental degradation.

  5. The moral responsibility of people in making economic choices "is often obscured by the existence of a complex series of relationships, rules, practices, ways of doing things, and patterns of behaviour."

D. Economic Structure

1. "We cannot abandon our moral responsibilities, even when it is difficult to fulfill them."
2. "We lose a sense of responsibility for those [economic] actions and decisions, thinking that whatever we choose to do is only a 'drop in the ocean.'"
3. "We accept that these 'economic realities' are somehow pre-ordained, rather than the result of human agency."
4. "The idea of bringing about a change in the economic system . . . begins to seem impossible."
5. "We transfer our responsibility to certain abstract concepts . . . rather than ourselves."
6. "When the Church considers the morality of an economic structure or of an economic decision, it is primarily interested in the impact of that structure or decision on people."
7. The central principles of Catholic social teaching can be applied well to globalization.

E. Christian Economic Values

1. We should avoid choices that "are not favorable to the good of the community as a whole, the common good."
2. "Solidarity is . . . a joining with others in a deep commitment to the common good."
3. "Economic actions and decisions must not only avoid harming the interests of the poor, but must actually contribute to their upliftment."
4. "The poor must be given privileged treatment, even at the cost of some measure of technical inefficiency."
5. Subsidiarity "holds that those things which can be done or decided at a lower level of society should not be taken over by a higher level."
6. "The way owners of property use their goods . . . must take into account the fact that they belong in the first instance to the community as a whole."
7. "We are called to a stewardship [of creation] which we have to exercise with due reverence and responsibility."
8. "Economic decisions must always take into account the interests of the people who will be affected by those decisions."

F. The South African Economy

1. "Christian justice demands that sufficient sharing takes place to ensure that the basic needs of all are met."
2. Half of the people in South Africa live in poverty and have no running water in their homes; one in six people live in shacks.
3. "By tolerating such high levels of poverty, the South African economy undermines the common good and fails to demonstrate the solidarity that our shared human dignity demands."
4. "A connection exists between high rates of unemployment and the distressingly high incidences of crime, family breakdown, domestic violence, gangsterism, and drug and alcohol abuse which beset our society."
5. "Material values should be accorded their proper place in relation to social, spiritual and moral values."
6. "An economy in which a significant proportion of the employed have little prospect of anything but a lifetime of unstimulating, low-paid mundane work, merely in order to survive, invites the social problems which we are currently experiencing."
7. "Women face a range of cultural, social and traditional barriers to their economic advancement. . . . Women are far more likely than men to be unemployed, to live in poverty and to lack marketable skills."
8. "An overwhelming proportion of the productive land in South Africa remains in the hands of the minority which obtained it historically by unjust means."
9. "Interest payments on the debt (which account for 22% of total government spending) accrue very largely, though by no means exclusively, to those who benefited most under apartheid."
10. Corruption is a "serious problem," taking the form of tax evasion, double invoicing, bribery, and theft of state property.

G. The World Economy

1. Globalization is "a positive and potentially beneficial trend" that at the present time "takes advantage of and exacerbates the inequalities between the nations."
2. The international community and the impacted states have a duty to mitigate the negative effects of globalization.
3. Policies of the World Bank and International Monetary Fund have "brought widespread suffering to the poor populations of developing countries."
4. In international trade, what rich countries "'give' to the developing world is generally only as much as they have to in order to gain access to new markets, to cheap labor, and to raw materials."

5. Unlimited economic growth is a myth: "It is simply impossible for the whole world to reach the material standard of living currently enjoyed by citizens of the richest nations."

H. What Can Be Done

1. "There are two major role players in setting economic policy–the government and the business community."
2. The 1996 South African Growth, Employment and Redistribution (GEAR) economic program has failed to meet its targets in economic growth, job creation, and redistribution of wealth.
3. "The tax burden on lower and middle-income earners [should] be reduced and balanced by an increase in estate duties and an increase in the top marginal rate applicable to the wealthiest sectors."
4. Privatization "leads to job losses and . . . to a deterioration in job quality."
5. "The business community has a deep responsibility to cooperate with government in pursuing such national goals as job creation, wealth distribution and the alleviation of poverty."
6. "It is not acceptable to create jobs with unacceptably low wages and poor working conditions."
7. "All workers . . . must consciously strive to work to the best of their ability."
8. Churches should "spread their social teachings more zealously, not as an optional extra, but as an integral and indispensable part of their overall message" to influence attitudes which, in turn, influence individual choices.

32

EVANGELIZATION IN MODERN DAY ASIA

First Plenary Assembly of the Federation of Asian Bishops' Conferences, 1974

> **Major Areas of Concern**
> —Signs of the Times
> —Local Church
> —Dialogue
> —The Poor
> —Renewal

The statement by the Federation of Asian Bishops' Conferences emphasizes that the task of evangelization in Asia goes on in a context of profound change and societal transformation. It sees the building up of the local church as the primary focus of evangelization. Central to the mission of the Church is the dialogue with other religions and with the poor. The Bishops see the dialogue with the poor as having consequences for the Church's commitment to justice.

HISTORICAL NOTE

The First Plenary Assembly of the FABC met in Taipei, Taiwan, in 1974. It chose as its theme "Evangelization," the same theme scheduled for the 1974 Synod of Bishops in Rome. The final statement reported the outcome of many workshops at the assembly.

I. Introduction
1. Modern day Asia is undergoing profound change: modernization, secularization, break-up of traditional society, industrialization (#4).
2. We need to read the "signs of the times" and assist in the promotion of human dignity and freedom (#'s 5–6).

II. Proclamation of the Gospel
In Jesus comes full meaning, liberation, community, and peace (#7).

A. Local Church
1. Primary focus of our evangelization is building up a truly local church (#9).
2. It is not an isolated church, but one incarnate with people, indigenous and inculturated (#'s 11–12).
3. It is in dialogue with the great religious traditions of Asian peoples (#'s 13–14).
4. This dialogue enriches our faith understanding, as well as offering to others the way of Jesus (#'s 16–18).

B. Dialogue with the Poor
1. In Asia, dialogue with people means dialogue with the poor (#19).
2. Poor are deprived and live under oppression from unjust social, economic, and political structures (#19).
3. Dialogue demands (#'s 20–21):
   a. experience of and sharing with the poor;
   b. commitment and effort to bring social justice.
4. Bishops affirm that work for justice is integral to preaching the Gospel and pledge support for those engaged in justice efforts (#'s 22–24).

III. Missionary Formation

A. Elements of Effective Proclamation
1. To preach Gospel is first to communicate experience of the Risen Lord (#30).

2. Contemplative spirit is needed in Asian context (#31).
3. Knowledge of Asian philosophies and ideologies and understanding of socio-economic factors are essential in education for mission in Asia (#32).
4. Genuine Asian theological reflection must be given priority (#33).

B. **Importance of Mass Media (#34)**

IV. **Conclusion**

1. Message to bearers of Gospel (#'s 35–42).
2. Prayer for blessings (#'s 43–50).

33

Journeying Together toward the Third Millennium

Statement of the Fifth Plenary Assembly of the Federation of Asian Bishops' Conferences, 1990

Major Areas of Concern
—Justice and Peace
—Modernization
—Dialogue and Participation
—Cultural Realities
—Structures of Sin
—Compassion

Journeying Together toward the Third Millennium begins by acknowledging that the challenge to the Church in Asia is to collaborate with people of good will in promoting justice, peace, and love. The document then lists several of the problems and injustices confronting Asian societies, including the breakdown of the nation-state system, massive poverty, and discrimination against women. The statement next calls on the churches in the region to a "joyful response" in working for liberation, development, and peace. *Journeying Together* concludes with a vision of a compassionate Church, always with the "weak and powerless," contemplative and simple in collaborating with other religious traditions in establishing God's Reign.

HISTORICAL NOTE

The Fifth Plenary Assembly of the Federation of Asian Bishops' Conferences issued this statement at the end of its 1990 convocation in Bandung, Indonesia. The bishops acknowledge the church's status as a minority partner in most Asian societies and craft a document that seeks to embody the spirit of the Church's social tradition in the contemplative context of Asian cultures and religious traditions. The statement builds on the social encyclicals of Pope John Paul II and previous statements of Asian bishops' conferences.

A. Introduction
1. "With the collapse of the Berlin Wall . . . we see an opportunity opening up for the Church to present its social doctrine" (#1.3).
2. "Our challenge is to proclaim the Good News of the Kingdom of God: to promote justice, peace, love, compassion, equality and brotherhood in these Asian realities" (#1.7).
3. "Our challenge is to cooperate with all people of goodwill in God's action in the world in the service of justice and peace" (#1.7).

B. Challenges and Hopes
1. "Change is the most constant factor in our societies" (#2.1.3).
2. "A striking change in many of our societies is the breakdown of the nation-state. Typically the nation-state in Asia was usually the creation of the colonial powers . . . It is not surprising that we now witness a variety of 'secessionist' movements and, tragically, widespread ethnic and communal conflict and violence" (#2.1.4).
3. "Modernization offers bright promise for our future [but] is fraught with ambiguity. . . . The beneficiaries of modernization are too often infected with secularism, materialism and consumerism" (#2.1.6).
4. "Within our context of change there is the unchanging reality of injustice," including massive poverty, environmental exploitation, militarization, discrimination against women, and economic desperation (#2.2.1).
5. "There is a new consciousness on the part of the marginalized that the situation is not an inevitable fate but something to be struggled against . . . [and] a new consciousness of solidarity—people are not isolated in the struggle" (#2.3.1).
6. "Dialogue between religious traditions, the ecological movement, and aspects of the women's movement offer hope for a more holistic spirituality" (#2.3.4).

7. "Desire for community goes together with desire for dialogue . . . [and] with desire for participation. . . . [This desire] is beginning to find its flowering in greater lay involvement in the Church's life and ministry" (#2.3.7).

8. "The movement in Asia toward modernity calls for a joyful response from the Church as it accompanies our Asian people, as partner with them in all positive movements of the human spirit" (#2.3.9).

C. **Mission and Mode in Contemporary Asia**

1. "Mission includes being with the people, responding to their needs, with sensitiveness to the presence of God in cultures and other religious traditions, and witnessing to the values of God's Kingdom through presence, solidarity, sharing and word" (#3.1.2).

2. "We evangelize because the Gospel is leaven for liberation and for the transformation of society. Our Asian world needs the values of the Kingdom and of Christ in order to bring about the human development, justice, peace and harmony with God, among peoples and with all creation" (#3.2.5).

3. "Mission in Asia will also seek through dialogue to serve the cause of unity of the peoples of Asia marked by such a diversity of beliefs, cultures and socio-political structures" (#4.2).

4. "In confrontation with Asian realities we have preached about values which ought to be pursued, but have often failed to follow through with effective actions that would help dismantle structures of sin oppressive of our peoples" (#4.5).

D. **The Role of the Church**

1. "The lay faithful should take upon themselves as their specific responsibility the renewal of Asian society according to the values of the Gospel" (#5.1).

2. "This calls for a thorough education of Catholics in the social doctrine of the Church, as well as the formation of their hearts toward just and compassionate living in present-day Asian society" (#5.2).

3. "It will be a compassion that makes the Church weak and powerless with those who are weak and powerless" (#6.4).

4. "This compassion will see even deeper, and will welcome in each human being—but especially the poor, deprived and oppressed—the very person of Christ" (#6.4).

5. There is an "indispensable necessity for the Church in Asia to be credible in its lifestyle and deeds in proclaiming its faith and in acting for justice and human rights" (#7.2).

6. "The Church, consistent with its social doctrine, [will] investi-

gate and remove from within its own structures and practices whatever obstructs human rights and justice" (#7.3.2.1).

7. "Specialized institutions [should] be set up to provide, from a faith-perspective, competence for lay persons in the socio-economic and political field" (#7.3.2.1).

8. "Episcopal conferences [should] incorporate into their Justice and Peace programs a vigorous defense and promotion of human rights, especially those of women and children, born and unborn" (#7.3.2.2).

9. "Episcopal conferences [should] develop and implement a program of forming men and women dedicated to the Gospel value of active non-violence, and facilitate the organization of peace groups" (#7.3.2.2).

10. "If people are convinced more by witnessing than by teaching, this is most true of the peoples of Asia whose cultures hold the contemplative dimension, renunciation, detachment, humility, simplicity and silence in the highest regard" (#9.2).

11. "A spirituality of harmony . . . expresses our intimate communion with God, our docility to his Spirit, our following of Jesus as we challenge the disharmonies of our Asian world. It moves us away from images of exterior organization, power or more secular effectiveness to images of simplicity, humble presence and service" (#9.5).

34

A Renewed Church in Asia: A Mission of Love and Service

Final Statement of the Seventh Plenary Assembly of the Federation of Asian Bishops' Conferences, 2000

Major Areas of Concern
—Globalization
—Empowerment
—Dialogue
—Renewal
—Democracy
—Ecology
—Militarization

A Renewed Church in Asia begins by stating several challenges facing the churches and societies in Asia, including globalization, exploitation and political strife. The document articulates a vision of renewal that features attentive listening, authentic empowerment and structural conversion. The statement then focuses on a number of pastoral concerns including discrimination against women, threats to the family and migration. *A Renewed Church in Asia* concludes by emphasizing that effective responses to these concerns will be integrated, collaborative and reflective of a "spirituality akin to the Asian soul."

HISTORICAL NOTE

An assembly whose composition was almost evenly divided between members of the hierarchy and other members of the church issued *A Renewed Church in Asia.* Of the 193 participants in the assembly held in January 2000 in Thailand, 5 were cardinals, 93 were bishops, and the rest were priests, religious, or lay people. The assembly was especially conscious of meeting at the dawning of the new millennium, yet also sought to craft a statement that was squarely in the tradition of Vatican II, the Special Assembly for Asia of the Synod of Bishops, and the six previous meetings of the Federation of Asian Bishops' Conferences.

Introduction
1. Christ was born of an Asian woman.
2. "For the poor, and especially for women, freedom, progress, globalization and other realities that now affect Asian peoples are not unmixed blessings."
3. "Globalization, unregulated by juridical and ethical norms, increases the millions who live below the poverty line."
4. In "Asian societies" there are "the caste system, dictatorships, exploitation of indigenous peoples, internal strife [and] widespread corruption."
5. "We dream of reconciliation between Asian brothers and sisters divided by wars and ethnic conflicts."

I. Renewal of the Church in Asia

A. A vision of a renewed Church in Asia includes:
1. "a Church of the Poor and a Church of the Young;"
2. "a Church indigenous and inculturated;"
3. "a deeply praying community;"
4. "an authentic community of faith;"
5. "a new sense of mission;"
6. "empowerment of men and women;"
7. "active involvement in generating and serving life;"
8. "triple dialogue with other faiths, with the poor and with cultures."

B. The Meaning of Renewal
1. "We need to be attentive to and open to the mysterious stirrings of the spirit in the realities of Asia and of the Church."
2. "We are a holy Church in need of purification."

3. Renewal "must include, given our human condition, not only conversion of minds and hearts but also a conversion of structures in which those marginalized by society are given a wider participation."

II. Issues and Challenges in the Mission of Love and Service

A. Globalization
1. "Marginalization and exclusion are [globalization's] direct consequences."
2. Globalization "has enabled only a small portion of the population to improve their standards of living, leaving many to remain in poverty."
3. "Globalization is an ethical and moral issue which we, as Church, can ill afford to ignore."

B. Fundamentalism
1. "Religious fundamentalism, or better, extremism . . . continues to bring division to Asian societies and suffering to our peoples."
2. "We must endeavor to promote the human rights of all people, regardless of caste, color, creed or religion."

C. Political Situation
1. In some situations there is "a hijacking of democracy . . . those who are elected pursue their own interests."
2. "Governments are forced to adopt policies and practices such as the Structural Adjustment Policies dictated by the International Monetary Fund, the World Bank, and the World Trade Organization. These policies are devoid of human face and social concern."

D. Ecology
1. "We see a steady, ongoing deterioration of our environment as a result of uncontrolled pollution, degrading poverty, deforestation, etc."
2. "Some Asian countries [have] become dumping grounds for toxic wastes, production platforms for hazardous industries, and industrialization proceeds without any environmental standards."

E. Militarization
1. "The increasing militarization of societies, fostered by governments and the 'death merchants,' is another challenge."
2. Major issues are "the banning of land mines, trade in small arms and nuclear proliferation."

III. The Challenge of Discerning the Asian Way

Introduction

1. "Asia is a cultural mosaic shining with its rich diversity. This is also true of the Catholic Church."
2. "We are committed to the emergence of the Asianness of the Church in Asia. This means that the Church has to be an embodiment of the Asian vision and values, especially interiority, harmony, a holistic and inclusive approach to every area of life."

A. Pastoral Concerns

1. "The new way of journeying with youth is to see the youth as resources and not as problems."
2. "There is widespread discrimination against the girl-child, destruction of the unborn girl-child, violence against and abuse of women and girls."
3. "We painfully witness the breakdown of the family in many places in our continent, especially in the urban centers."
4. The right of indigenous people "to land is threatened; their fields are laid bare; they themselves are subjected to economic exploitation, excluded from political participation and reduced to the status of second class citizens."
5. "People migrate within Asia and from Asia to other continents for many reasons, among them poverty, war and ethnic conflicts, the denial of human rights and fundamental freedoms."

B. Our Response

1. Our approach must be "integrated," "collaborative," and "empowering."
2. Formation of all church members "should promote a profound understanding of the elements of prayer and spirituality akin to the Asian soul."
3. "The Church's task of promoting justice, peace and human development, as well as safeguarding human rights, will be more effective when policy-makers, planners and executives are properly informed about the human and moral side of their professional career or service."
4. "Based on the ethical and moral imperatives that are found in the social teaching of the Church, the process of advocacy should be articulated effectively" with an "emphasis on the common good."

35

A MILESTONE FOR THE HUMAN FAMILY

Pastoral Letter of the Catholic Bishops of Australia to Mark the 50th Anniversary of the Universal Declaration of Human Rights, 1998

Major Areas of Concern
—Human Rights
—Social Obligations
—Women and Poverty
—Development and Evangelization

A Milestone for the Human Family celebrates the fiftieth anniversary of the Universal Declaration of Human Rights and offers a reflection on this document in light of Roman Catholic tradition and the Australian experience. *A Milestone* begins by noting that in the fifty years since the issuance of the Universal Declaration there has been significant progress in recognizing these rights, but poverty and injustice are still too prevalent and pervasive. The pastoral letter points out the church's substantial teaching on human rights and the way it has related these rights to justice, development, and peace. *A Milestone* notes the challenges particular rights face for their fulfillment in the context of Australian society and concludes with several reflections on human rights, Australia and the Catholic Church.

HISTORICAL NOTE

A Milestone for the Human Family is concerned with history: commemorating the fiftieth anniversary of one of the most important documents in the human tradition and reflecting on the rights espoused in this document in light of the Catholic tradition. The pastoral letter notes the progress that was made between 1948 and 1998 in the recognition and implementation of human rights. *A Milestone* also sketches the contributions various popes have made to the cause of human rights, beginning with Pope Leo XIII and the body of modern Catholic social teaching that he began.

I. The Declaration

1. Recognition of human dignity and equal, inalienable human rights for all is the foundation of freedom, justice and peace.
2. The most fundamental of the rights enumerated in the Declaration are the right to life, freedom and full participation in society.
3. Other rights that flow from these rights include political, civil, economic, social, and cultural rights which, collectively, constitute "the right to be free from the burden of poverty and sociological disadvantage."
4. These rights are universal and indivisible: the economic, social and cultural rights are just as essential as civil and political rights. All human rights must be rooted in each culture and established juridically.

II. Human Rights Since 1948

1. During the past half century, the world has experienced much progress and a growing consensus in recognition of these rights.
2. Progress includes the end of colonialism and many corrupt and tyrannical regimes of the Left and the Right, the demise of apartheid, lack of a global war, mass movements against discrimination, advances made by the women's movement, technological advancements and growing awareness of human rights.
3. However, there is still too much injustice and serious violations of basic rights: e.g. genocide, poverty, hunger, illiteracy, abortion, discrimination, torture, and slavery.
4. Absolute poverty afflicts 1.3 million people. Millions of others suffer in poverty, including thousands of refugees.
5. Regional wars continue. "Women and children are in the clear majority of those who suffer most from the effects of war, poverty, discrimination, and other forms of injustice and abuse."

6. Technological advances give rise to grave moral, human rights and justice issues around genetics and euthanasia.

III. The Catholic Church and the Human Rights Movement

1. Beginning with Pope Leo XIII, the Church has championed the rights of the oppressed and the disadvantaged through Catholic social teaching.
2. Pope John XXIII moved the Church from a cautious approach to the UN and its Declaration to one of strong support.
3. *Peace on Earth (Pacem in Terris)* resembles the Universal Declaration with new points of emphasis:
   a. the right to own property is limited by social obligations;
   b. rights are always related to corresponding social obligations and could be limited by demands of the common good.
4. Vatican II "reaffirmed and developed" the Church's teaching on human rights by emphasizing religious liberty and affirming human dignity.
5. Pope Paul VI, through formation of the Pontifical Council for Justice and Peace and the emphasis on development in *Populorum Progressio* and the 1971 World Synod of Bishops, tied rights to justice and peace.
6. Pope John Paul II has "emphasized repeatedly" the "central place of human rights, social justice and the promotion of peace in the Church's mission."

IV. Australia and Human Rights

1. The human community "should ensure that Australia's commitment to human rights here and abroad is maintained and improved."
2. The Australian Catholic Church's commitment to human rights predated the Universal Declaration with the publication of the first Social Justice Sunday statement in 1940.
3. Since Vatican II, the Australian Catholic Bishops have created eight agencies and commissions to promote human rights and justice and peace. Religious communities have established even more.
4. Human rights issues of particular concern for Australia include human life issues, unemployment, racism, sexism, immigration, government policy and actions towards refugees, the treatment and rights of Aborigines and Torres Strait Islanders, domestic violence, environmental degradation, rural poverty, industrial relations, prisons and tax inequities.

V. Matters for Reflection

1. While animals, plants and even future generations of human beings may not "have rights in the strict sense . . . our obligations in this area are serious and increasingly recognized today."
2. "Freedom does not mean libertarianism for we have duties as well as rights."
3. The Church respects responsible free expression, but will oppose any legislation that would force religious bodies to act against their principles.
4. The Catholic Church supports the Universal Declaration's statement that the family "is the natural and fundamental unit of society" (Article 16, sub-section 3). Religious, ethnic and indigenous groups also possess human rights collectively.
5. In an era of globalization, national sovereignty should not be undermined, though global institutions such as the International Criminal Court are needed.
6. "While globalization can bring benefits to the human race, it also opens the way to serious abuses and to the possibility of exploitation of resources." Healthy globalization requires the Catholic social principles of solidarity, the common good and subsidiarity.
7. The right to life is the "most fundamental" human right but it has been "ignored and transgressed" in many countries through genocide, civilian massacres in war, abortion, euthanasia, capital punishment, and innumerable deaths, especially of children from malnutrition, preventable illness and oppression.
8. "The Bishops of Australia would certainly oppose any move to re-introduce the death penalty in this country."
9. Women's rights are human rights. The human rights of women and girls continue to be violated by the use of rape in war, reduced food, education and healthcare, and human trafficking.

VI. Conclusion

1. "There is a close link between the Church's mission of evangelization and its defense and promotion of human rights."
2. "An integral part of Catholics' celebration of the Jubilee [Year of 2000] should be a deepening of awareness of the Church's teaching on social justice" and of the need to apply it to human rights issues at home and abroad.

36

THE COMMON GOOD AND THE CATHOLIC CHURCH'S SOCIAL TEACHING

Catholic Bishops' Conference of England and Wales, 1996

Major Areas of Concern
—Catholic Social Teaching
—Common Good
—Subsidiarity
—Solidarity
—Political Responsibility
—Structures of Sin
—Democracy and Human Rights

The Common Good and the Catholic Church's Social Teaching begins by noting the contribution that Church social teaching can make to the national political debate. The statement emphasizes solidarity and subsidiarity and the role of these concepts in promoting the common good. The document then identifies a series of important concerns facing the nation and the nation's desire to impact the world for the good. These issues include the right to life, the gap between the rich and the poor, and fair and equitable development. The statement concludes by challenging the British people to reclaim the common good as the national purpose.

HISTORICAL NOTE

The Catholic Bishops' Conference of England and Wales issued *The Common Good and the Catholic Church's Social Teaching* in 1996 to spark public debate in anticipation of the coming general election. The bishops were cognizant of opinion surveys that showed a significant mood of pessimism sweeping the nation. The bishops write squarely within the universal tradition of Catholic social teaching, presumably hoping to inspire citizens to embrace the concept of the common good and its twin pillars of solidarity and subsidiarity.

I. Christian Citizens in Modern Britain

A. The Church and Catholic Social Teaching
1. "Leaders of the Church have to be careful not to step outside the limits of their own competence nor to infringe the proper autonomy of lay people. It is not for bishops to tell people how to vote" (#2).
2. Catholic social teachings "represent a formidable body of insight and guidance" (#3).
3. Catholic social teaching "is more relevant than it has ever been to the complex problems faced by advanced Western countries" (#4).
4. The Church has "a deep involvement in the public life of Britain" including "a major stake in welfare and education provision" (#7).
5. "The Catholic social vision has as its focal point the human person" (#12).
6. "Christ challenges us to see his presence in our neighbour, especially the neighbour who suffers or who lacks what is essential to human flourishing" (#12).
7. "Policies which treat people as only economic units, or policies which reduce people to a passive state of dependency on welfare, do not do justice to the dignity of the human person" (#13).
8. "People who are poor and vulnerable have a special place in Catholic teaching: this is what is meant by the 'preferential option for the poor'. . . . The poor are not a burden; they are our brothers and sisters" (#14).

B. Solidarity, Subsidiarity and Society
1. "Solidarity with our neighbour is also about the promotion of equality of rights and equality of opportunities; hence we must oppose all forms of discrimination and racism" (#14).
2. "An insight of Christian faith in the Trinity is the knowledge that the desire to belong to human society is God-given.

Human beings are made in the image of God, and within the one God is a divine society of three Persons" (#18).

3. "There are ways of structuring society which are inimical to human progress and personal development. The Church calls them 'structures of sin'" (#19).

4. "There are other ways of structuring society which facilitate true human development and correspond to moral principles and demands. . . . A well constructed society will be one that gives priority to the integrity, stability and health of family life" (#21).

5. "In a centralized society, subsidiarity will mainly mean passing power downwards; but it can also mean passing appropriate powers upwards" (#22).

6. "If subsidiarity is the principle behind the organization of societies from a vertical perspective, solidarity is the equivalent horizontal perspective" (#23).

7. "The general purpose of the Church's social teaching is to contribute to the formation of conscience as a basis for specific action. . . . It is for individuals and groups to decide how best to apply it in particular circumstances" (#27).

C. The Catholic Social Tradition

1. "Social teaching is not limited to a collection of official, mainly papal texts. It is an oral tradition as well as a written one, and it is a lived and living tradition. Many Catholics whose lives are dedicated to the service and welfare of others make this teaching present by their very activity, even if they have never read a social encyclical" (#28).

2. "In the course of the last hundred years the focus of attention of these documents has gradually extended from Western Europe to the whole globe" (#29).

3. "As bishops, we hope to see more participation in the future development of Catholic Social Teaching, so that it is properly owned by all Catholics" (#31).

4. "The development of Catholic teaching in the past has inevitably reflected particular historical circumstances. . . . At certain times it has even been wrongly invoked in support of oppressive regimes or governments perpetrating social injustice" (#32).

5. "Britain has a mature political culture and democratic tradition. . . . These institutions have been admired all over the world" (#33).

6. "The Church's teaching now fully embraces two fundamental features of modern society about which it once had some difficulties: democracy and human rights" (#34).

7. "If democracy is not to become a democratic tyranny in which the majority oppresses the minority, it is necessary for the pub-

lic to have an understanding of the common good and the concepts that underlie it" (#35).

8. "Individuals have a claim on each other and on society for certain basic minimum conditions without which the value of human life is diminished or even negated" (#36).

9. "Rights are universal. . . . All flow from the one fundamental right: the right to life" (#37).

10. "Catholic Social Teaching sees an intimate relationship between social and political liberation on the one hand, and on the other, the salvation to which the Church calls us in the name of Jesus Christ" (#39).

D. **Individuals and the Common Good**

1. "One of the most important steps in the evangelization of the social order is the freeing of individuals from the inertia and passivity that comes from oppression, hopelessness or cynicism" (#40).

2. Catholics should reflect on the principles and applications of Church social teaching in the "traditional Catholic custom of 'examination of conscience'" (#41).

3. Catholic teachers and preachers must "avoid giving the impression that observance of [Catholic social] teaching is optional for Catholics" (#42).

4. The current tendency in Catholic social teaching "is to integrate it with the rest of the Church's moral teaching" (#43).

5. Catholic social teaching "frequently uses natural law and Biblical sources alongside each other, for mutual elucidation" (#47).

6. "Common good is the whole network of social conditions which enable human individuals and groups to flourish and live a fully, genuinely human life, otherwise described as 'integral human development'" (#48).

7. Subsidiarity "supports a dispersal of authority as close to the grass roots as good government allows, and it prefers local over central decision-making" (#52).

8. Solidarity "is above all a question of interdependence . . . a firm and persevering determination to commit oneself to the common good" (#53).

II. Application to Contemporary Questions

A. **The Political Vocation**

1. Catholic social teaching should not "be allowed to remain at the level of broad generalities in order to avoid controversy" (#54).

2. "There are trends in British society and political life which seem to us to be contrary to Catholic teaching, as well as features of public and private morality which are commendable" (#54).
3. "There is a strong Christian tradition of public service in all the major British parties" (#57).
4. "Politics is an honourable vocation which often exacts great personal cost from those who engage in it" (#58).
5. "An attitude of cynicism towards those engaged in public life is one of those tendencies against which we feel we must speak out" (#59).
6. "One of the most important questions an elector has to enquire into at an election is . . . about the attitude and character of each candidate" (#63).

B. **Specific Issues in the General Election**

1. "In the three decades since the passage of the Abortion Act, human life has been devalued to the extent where abortion is widely regarded as a remedy for any social or personal difficulties" (#66).
2. "The foundations of medical ethics [must be] securely rooted in respect for human life at all its stages" (#68).
3. There is "a point at which the scale of the gap between the very wealthy and those at the bottom range of income begins to undermine the common good" (#70).
4. "The Church's social teaching can be summed up as the obligation of every individual to contribute to the good of society, in the interests of justice and in pursuit of the 'option for the poor'" (#73).
5. "The first duty of the citizen toward the common good is to ensure that nobody is marginalized . . . and to bring back into . . . the community those who have been marginalised" (#75).
6. "The Church recognizes that market forces, when properly regulated in the name of the common good, can be an efficient mechanism for matching resources to needs in a developed society" (#78).
7. "Those who advocate unlimited free-market capitalism and at the same time lament the decline in public and private morality, to which the encouragement of selfishness is a prime contributing factor, must ask themselves whether the messages they are sending are in fact mutually contradictory" (#80).

C. **The Common Good**

1. "It is always the business of public authority to arbitrate between the sometimes conflicting demands of a market economy and the common good" (#81).

2. "The search for profit must not be allowed to override all other moral considerations" (#83).
3. "Those most likely to suffer from over-reliance on competition . . . are the poor, vulnerable, powerless and defenseless. . . . Unlimited free markets tend to produce what is, in effect, an 'option against the poor'" (#85).
4. "There seems to be a decline in regard for the common good in [the newspaper and broadcasting] industry" (#88).
5. "Work increases the common good" (#90).
6. Rights of workers include "the right to decent work, to just wages, to security of employment" among other rights (#91).

D. Britain, Europe and the Global Common Good

1. "The principle of subsidiarity applies particularly to Britain's relations with the European Union, especially the extent to which social, financial and monetary decisions ought to be made" (#99).
2. "The universal common good is violated if there are places anywhere in the world where basic needs like clean water, food, shelter, health care, education and livelihood are not available to all or if the rights and dignity of all are not respected" (#102).
3. "The debt burden is a major factor in perpetuating poverty" (#104).
4. "International cooperation and regulation are needed to protect weak and vulnerable countries in their transition to full participation in the global economy" (#105).
5. "Solidarity of the human family will also require the developed world to restrict the promotion of arms sales to poor countries" (#105).
6. "Care for the environment is part of care for the common good" (#106).

E. Conclusion

1. "The economy exists for the human person, not the other way around" (#111).
2. "'Downsizing' is a prevalent cause of social injustice in modern society" (#112).
3. "The nation's real crisis is not economic, but spiritual and moral" (#113).
4. "This crisis concerns loss of individual belief and confusion over personal moral behaviour. . . . [People] seem to be losing their faith in the possibility of a better future" (#114).
5. "The loss of confidence in the concept of the common good is one of the primary factors behind the national mood of pes-

simism. It betrays a weakening of the sense of mutual responsibility and a decline in the spirit of solidarity" (#116).

6. The political arena has to be reclaimed in the name of the common good. . . . Solidarity and subsidiarity need to be applied systematically to the reform of the institutions of public life" (#119).

PART FOUR

STUDY GUIDES

1

SUGGESTED USES

WHO CAN BENEFIT

This book will be useful to many individuals and groups interested in discovering the rich tradition of social teaching in the Catholic Church during recent times:

—social concern committees and ministry groups exploring the foundations of their mission,
—solidarity organizations and other issue-directed groups researching the Church's tradition of teaching on a particular issue or problem,
—post-RENEW Groups and adult education programs,
—university and college classes,
—high school religion classes and "service" programs,
—teacher education programs.

HOW TO USE

A number of creative uses for this book will undoubtedly arise as groups clarify their own purposes for undertaking a study of Catholic social teaching. Study groups might want to initiate their planning by (1) discerning their own purposes or directions for exploration and (2) choosing a discussion format consistent with their particular needs. The authors would like to suggest one possible format for the study of these documents.

A facilitator might divide each study session into three phases:

A. **The Descriptive Phase:** Discuss the group's understanding of the content of the document in question. Ask:
   1. What content seems most familiar to participants based on their understanding of the faith?

2. What is new to them?
3. What was/is the historical situation to which this text is responding?
4. What is the most striking part of the document? Why?

B. **The Critical Phase:** Relate the document to the participants' experiences. Let the document critique their experience and, in turn, let their experience critique the document. The study questions for each document have been framed to facilitate this process. Suggest other questions as well.

C. **The Action Phase:** Explore the action possibilities that the document suggests keeping the particular needs of the group in mind.

A NOTE ON THE ORDER OF THE DOCUMENTS

The documents are divided into *Documents to the Universal Church* and *Documents to Regional Churches.* In past editions all the outlines were provided in their chronological order. Historical study has the following advantages: it illustrates the development of concepts, including changes in language and approach; it highlights the historical relativity of the documents (these are responses to particular sets of circumstances); and it encourages us to be creative rather than imitative in applying the Gospel and the Church's teachings in our own situations. Regional overviews are also important to see how Catholic social teaching relates to the "signs of the times" in different parts of the world.

Since there are 36 documents in this edition, two divisions are provided. The universal documents are listed according to chronological order while the regional documents are listed by chronological order within their geographic region.

It will be helpful to read the introductory chapters that explain more about the inter-relatedness of the documents. They are all a part of a rich and dynamic cross-fertilization of Catholic social teaching.

2

DISCUSSION QUESTIONS

Part One: Historical Background

INTRODUCTION

1. What has been your own understanding of the Church's social teachings?
2. Has this understanding influenced you?
3. How important is it for you to have the guidance of the Church's teachings in social matters?
4. What seems to be the major consensus of the Church in regard to social justice questions?

MAJOR LESSONS OF CATHOLIC SOCIAL TEACHING

1. Are you familiar with some of these lessons?
2. Why are these considered central to Catholic social teaching?
3. Are there other tenets you would add to the list?

Part Two: Documents to the Universal Church

ON THE CONDITION OF LABOR

1. The working conditions that inspired this document reflected the images of Charles Dickens's British factories where workers toiled in horrible conditions. From your experience or knowledge, do similar conditions still exist? What principles of this encyclical still apply?

2. What is the condition of workers and their unions in your own country? Are their basic rights upheld? What are conditions of workers in other parts of the world?
3. How does the concept of human dignity relate to the rights of workers and those in poverty?
4. What are the Church and your government doing to improve the situation of workers and the poor? How can you or your group contribute to efforts to change unjust structures?

THE RECONSTRUCTION OF THE SOCIAL ORDER

1. Why does the Church have a right and a duty to speak on social issues?
2. Discuss the weaknesses of capitalism and socialism in light of Catholic social teaching.

CHRISTIANITY AND SOCIAL PROGRESS

1. This document notes the new developments between 1931 and 1961. What, in your view, are the significant developments that have occurred in the world since then?
2. Name ways in which these new developments affect your life and the life of your community.
3. How do you define your role as a Christian in the world?

PEACE ON EARTH

1. In 1963, Pope John XXIII listed significant "signs of the times." What would you add to (or subtract from) that list today?
2. For you and your community, what are the most important rights that Pope John XXIII listed? Explain.
3. Analyze the peace efforts of your community from the perspective of this encyclical.

THE CHURCH IN THE MODERN WORLD

1. What are the most important "joys and hopes, sorrows and anxieties" of our contemporary world? Which ones affect you and your church community the most?
2. Freud referred to religion's function as "illusion"; Marx as "ideology." In what way do you think religion should function in the human community?

3. Should the Church respond to the agenda of the world? What does this mean in practical terms?
4. List what you believe are the major things that people need in order to realize their dignity. What factors in your community contribute to, or hinder, the achievement of this dignity?

THE DEVELOPMENT OF PEOPLES

1. Have you experienced solidarity with people of other areas or nations? Discuss.
2. How should our nation be guided in its relations with poorer nations?
3. Efforts at "development" by wealthier nations have not always benefited the poorer nations. What do you know about the major pitfalls of development efforts to date?
4. What does the "preferential option for the poor" mean to you?

A CALL TO ACTION

1. Think of one unjust structure or system in your nation that you would like to change. How can you and the members of your community act to bring about this change?
2. How do you and your church community respond to the challenge of this document to reflect on the contemporary situation, to apply Gospel principles, and to take political actions when appropriate? Do you have a process in place to do this? Can you create one?

JUSTICE IN THE WORLD

1. Name the major reasons that prompt you to work for justice. List factors in your country that foster such work for justice and factors that hinder it.
2. Discuss how your faith in Jesus encourages you to do more for justice and peace?

EVANGELIZATION IN THE MODERN WORLD

1. Share with the other members of your group the spiritual journey that has led you to be concerned about justice and peace. What were your experiences on this journey?
2. This document states that the witness of a truly Christian life is needed for effective evangelization. What impressions do outsiders have of your local Christian community? What examples do you want your community to provide?

ON HUMAN WORK

1. Illustrate, by way of examples from your own work situation or others, what the "priority of labor over capital" means to you.
2. In what ways does your own work give you a sense of dignity?
3. What aspects of your daily work affirm your dignity? Which are dehumanizing?
4. The complexity of today's world inhibits some people from social involvement. How do you deal with such complexity? How do others you know, or know of, deal with it?

THE SOCIAL CONCERNS OF THE CHURCH

1. Why is Pope John Paul II critical of *both* liberal capitalism and Marxist collectivism?
2. Has the socio-economic life of people in the rich countries of the world improved in the past twenty years? Of people in the poor countries?
3. Why is "development" more than simply economic progress? What is "authentic human development"?
4. What "structures of sin" could you name in the present global situation?

THE CHURCH AND RACISM

1. Why does our Christian faith reject racism?
2. What are some of the ways that racism has been a part or our communities? What can you or your community do about it?

THE MISSIONARY ACTIVITY OF THE CHURCH

1. What are aspects of the "proclamation of Christ" that relate to human dignity?
2. What are ways to "inculturate" the Gospel, that is, to make the Gospel more effective in the culture of this country and of other countries?

ONE HUNDRED YEARS

1. Why did Pope John Paul II think that the fall of Marxism in Eastern Europe was *not* a victory for the market economies?
2. What are some of the responsibilities the Pope believes the richer nations have toward the poorer ones? What are some ways your nation can deal with economic injustices in other countries?
3. What are some things your parish or school could do to help form human minds and hearts for justice and peace?

CATECHISM

1. What does the Catechism emphasize in articulating the social teachings of the Church?
2. What is the relationship between private and public contributions to the common good? Why are both necessary for a just world and a just society?
3. What economic values are highlighted in the Catechism? Do they differ from the economic tenets you hear about in the media, in our culture, in our government policies? What are the central differences?
4. What are the proactive and positive actions the Catechism recommends to promote God's peace in the human community?

THE GOSPEL OF LIFE

1. What are the economic, political, and cultural forces in the modern world that threaten respect for all life?
2. What are the "signs of hope" in the modern world that indicate respect for all life and for the gift of creation?
3. What does a "consistent ethic of life" mean? Discuss the challenges of committing to a concept of a "seamless garment." Discuss ways to be a witness in the face of so many problems that threaten life at all stages.

WORLD CONFERENCE AGAINST RACISM

1. Why does the Vatican stress the importance of forgiveness when speaking about discrimination? What does the process of forgiveness consist of?
2. What kinds of educational experience help to defeat racism?
3. Why is affirmative action condoned and what limits are put on it?

Part Three: Documents to the Regional Churches

A. NORTH AMERICA

BROTHERS AND SISTERS TO US

1. What are some ways that your parish or school can assist the process of conversion and renewal to change unjust systems and structures that support racism?
2. What are some goals of racial justice that we should work for?

THE CHALLENGE OF PEACE

1. How is the Old Testament notion of war and peace changed by the life and actions of Jesus?
2. What elements of U.S. defense policy did the bishops condemn in this document? What elements did they accept? What is the situation today and how are the U.S. bishops responding to it?
3. What steps do the bishops propose that the United States take to work actively toward peace?

THE HISPANIC PRESENCE

1. What are some of the conditions that create situations of "pervasive poverty" for so many Hispanics in the United States? What must be challenged in order to help them?
2. What are a few concrete things the U.S. Church can do to assist the Latin American Church?

ECONOMIC JUSTICE FOR ALL

1. Has the U.S. economy helped you and your family to live a fully human life? How has the economy hindered your efforts? In what ways do you think the U.S. economic structure helps or hinders those in poverty?
2. What are some of the major principles the bishops suggest to help us shape a more just economy? List those principles that you consider to be the most important.
3. Why do the bishops become very specific in their policy recommendations to meet economic problems?

TO THE ENDS OF THE EARTH

1. What are the major elements of the Church's understanding of itself as "missionary"?
2. What are the principal components of the missionary task as outlined in this document?
3. What can individuals and communities do to promote the Church's missionary activity?

THE STRUGGLE AGAINST POVERTY

1. How is the Canadian Bishops' Pastoral Letter shaped by Vatican II and papal teaching? How is it specific to Canada, and how does it relate to a wider reality in the world?

2. Why is the "eradication" of poverty the focus of the letter, rather than charity toward the poor? How are these related? How are they different?

3. Why do the bishops believe that "solving the problem of poverty among women is the key to eliminating poverty in Canada?" What are possible solutions to poverty among women?

4. The bishops call Christians to denounce "social sin." Give some examples of what you would consider social sin. What are effective ways to denounce such sins?

5. How do the Canadian bishops define solidarity? Are any of their definitions new to you? How do these definitions expand your own understanding of being in solidarity with all your sisters and brothers?

STRANGERS NO LONGER—MEXICO/U.S.

1. Why are bishops from both countries concerned about Mexican migration to the United States? Why do you think they chose to issue a joint statement?

2. How does the image of Jesus, Mary, and Joseph as refugees speak to Christians today?

3. What are rights that the bishops call to our attention? How can these rights be balanced?

B. CENTRAL AND LATIN AMERICA

THE MEDELLÍN CONFERENCE DOCUMENTS

1. What are the ways in which the bishops ground their recommendations for Latin American society in the Church's social teaching?

2. What aspects of Latin American society did the bishops recommend changing? Are these still problems in the region?

3. In what ways can the injustice in Latin America cause a lack of justice and peace on the entire continent? What should this mean for U.S. policy in that region?

THE PUEBLA CONFERENCE DOCUMENT

1. What do the Latin American bishops see as the proper role of the Church in the world? Why did they suggest this particular role?

2. On what principles does evangelization rest?

3. How are the option for the poor and liberation related to evangelization and base communities?

JOURNEYING IN CENTRAL AMERICA

1. What problems related to migration are the bishops concerned with? Compare and contrast this document with the *Strangers No Longer* letter from the Mexican/U.S. bishops.
2. How are these concerns related to their statement on free trade agreements and development in their region?

HUNGER IN BRAZIL

1. The bishops of Brazil are very specific in their critique of a for-profit, market economy and its impact on those in poverty. Review their concerns and discuss how they are related to the basic tenets of Catholic social teaching.
2. The bishops make the point that the cause of hunger is the unjust distribution of food and wealth, not a scarcity of food. What do the Brazilian bishops emphasize in dealing with the challenge of "too much" and "too little" resources occurring at the same time?
3. How would the business of food production and distribution change if the bishops' words were heeded?

C. AFRICA

JUSTICE AND EVANGELIZATION IN AFRICA

1. What factors, both internal and external, do you think have been influential in shaping Africa today?
2. What does it mean to refer to the family as the "first school of justice"? How can this happen in Africa and elsewhere?

THE FUTURE IS OURS—ZAMBIA

1. The Zambian bishops call for more responsibility and respect from citizens, as well as a spirit of service and accountability in the government. Why are all these important to a just society? Can you give specific examples of the presence or absence of these traits in your country and/or in other countries?
2. From the perspective of Catholic social teaching, why is it crucial as an economic priority that investment should generate jobs? Is job creation a priority in your local, regional, and national government policy? Why or why not?
3. Share what you know about the problems of external debt and the

efforts of many groups to help those suffering under the burden of unjust debt.

ECONOMIC JUSTICE IN SOUTH AFRICA

1. The South African bishops stress the moral quality of economies and the moral responsibility of people in making economic choices. What do they warn us about in these areas?
2. How do the bishops define Christian economic values?
3. What main points do they present about the world economy? How can you learn more about these specific injustices?
4. The bishops stress job creation, just wages, and working conditions. Why have these concerns been ignored so often in history? Why must they constantly be reemphasized by people of faith?

D. Asia

EVANGELIZATION IN MODERN DAY ASIA

1. What is your experience of "local church" as a reality in your area? Is an outreach in evangelization part of your church's mission?
2. If you were to work for greater dialogue with those in poverty in your area, what would this require? How would everyone involved benefit?

JOURNEYING TOGETHER—ASIA

1. Identify themes in this statement that were discussed by Pope John Paul II in his encyclicals.
2. What are some aspects of modernization to which the Asian bishops are responding?
3. How does this document define "mission"? What aspect of this definition of mission challenges you?
4. What specific roles for the Church in Asia are suggested by the bishops? What are cultural aspects of Asia that they incorporate into their suggestions?
5. In Asia, Christianity is a minor religious force. How do the bishops expect Asian Christians to meet this challenge?

A RENEWED CHURCH IN ASIA

1. Compare and contrast the views on globalization in this document with the documents from other regions.

2. What does renewal mean to the Asian bishops? What would it mean for your local and regional church communities to go through a renewal?

E. Australia

A MILESTONE FOR THE HUMAN FAMILY

1. What is the difference to both the giver and the receiver between respecting a person's right to food and providing food as a gesture of charity?
2. What are pressing problems the Australian bishops mention as they seek to promote human rights in their country? Compare and contrast these with issues in other countries.
3. This letter mentions that while globalization can bring benefits, it has opened the way for serious abuses and exploitation. What are some examples of these?
4. Discuss why the bishops believe that solidarity, the common good, and subsidiarity have a "particular relevance" to globalization.

F. Europe

THE COMMON GOOD—ENGLAND AND WALES

1. How are "structures of sin" defined? Can you give examples of specific structures or systems, formal or informal, past and present, where injustice is embedded into the social, legal, and governmental structure?
2. How do the bishops define "well-constructed societies" and the just structures and systems they promote?
3. Catholic social teaching is described as a "lived and living tradition," with Catholics making this teaching present "by their very activity." Can you identify those who do (or have done so) by their activities?
4. What would our churches, schools, universities, and small faith communities be like if Catholic social teaching were "properly owned" and developed by all members of the Church?
5. What concerns do the bishops of the developed countries of Europe share with the bishops from developing countries, known as the "South"?

3

WHERE TO FIND
THE DOCUMENTS

Many documents are currently available on web sites. This is a partial list of where to find documents and can be used to start the search process.

Vatican: The documents outlined and discussed in Part II, chapters 1–7, 9–11, and 13–17 are available on the Vatican's web site: *www.vatican.va*. O'Brien and Shannon's book, listed in the bibliography, contains many of the documents to the Universal Church. Document 8, Justice in the World, and other documents are available on the web site of the Archdiocese of St. Paul and Minneapolis Office of Social Justice: *www.osjspm.org/cst*. Document 12 is available on the web site of the St. Joseph Church, Milton, Louisiana: *www.stjo-milton.org/current/racism*.

United States: Documents 19, 22, and 24 are available on the web site of the United States Conference of Catholic Bishops (USCCB): *www.usccb.org*. Documents 18 and 21 are on the web site of the Archdiocese of St. Paul and Minneapolis Office of Social Justice: *www.osjspm.org/cst*. All of the documents can be obtained from the USCCB at 3211 4th Street, N.E., Washington, D.C. 20017-1194.

Canada: The Canadian document is available from the Canadian Catholic Conference of Bishops' web site: *www.cccb.ca* or by contacting CCCB Publications, Canadian Conference of Catholic Bishops, 2500 Don Reid Drive, Ottawa (Ontario), K1H 2J2 Canada.

Central America and Latin America: The Medellín document is available at: *http://www.shc.edu/theolibrary/cstdocs.htm*. Both Medellín and Puebla conference documents are in Documents 16 and 18 in the bibliography. The Brazilian document is available (in Portuguese, 2003) from Paulinas, Rua Pedro de Toledo, 164, 04039-000 Sao Paulo-SP, Brazil.

Africa: The African documents are available on the web site of the Center of Concern, 1225 Otis St. N.E., Washington D.C. 20017-2516. Web site: *www.coc.org.*

Asia: For copies of the Asian documents, contact Claretian Communications, Inc.; #8 Mayumi St.; U.P.P.O. Box 4, Diliman; 1101 Quezon City, Philippines, or through the internet at *www.bible.claret.org.*

Australia: The Australian document is available on the Australian Bishops' Conference web site: *www.catholic.org.au.*

England: The document from England is available on the web site of the Catholic Church of England and Wales: *www.catholic-ew.org.uk/frameset.htm* and also *www.osjspm.org/cst* or from Gabriel Communications Ltd, 1st Floor, St James's Buildings, Oxford Street, Manchester M1 6FP, England.

BIBLIOGRAPHY

1. Antoncich, Ricardo. *Christians in the Face of Injustice: Toward a Latin American Reading of the Church's Social Teaching.* Maryknoll, N.Y.: Orbis Books, 1987.
> A very perceptive interpretation of the social message from the perspective of the Christian struggle in Latin America; especially helpful in the view of private property.

2. Baum, Gregory. *The Priority of Labor.* New York: Paulist Press, 1982.
> Commentary on John Paul II's *On Human Labor,* with profound explanation of new orientations of Catholic social teaching.

3. Baum, Gregory. *Theology and Society.* New York: Paulist Press, 1987.
> An insightful book that relates Catholic social teaching to liberation theology, political theology, and the North American social context.

4. Baum, Gregory, and Ellsberg, Robert, eds. *The Logic of Solidarity.* Maryknoll, N.Y.: Orbis Books, 1989.
> An excellent series of commentaries on *Sollicitudo Rei Socialis.*

5. Benestad, James, and Butler, Frank, eds. *A Quest for Justice: A Compendium of Statements of the U.S. Bishops on the Political and Social Order, 1966–1980.* Washington, D.C.: United States Catholic Conference, 1981.
> Complete collection of major statements by the U.S. bishops on a variety of topics.

6. Berry, Thomas, C.P., with Clark, Thomas, S.J. *Befriending the Earth.* Mystic, Conn.: Twenty-Third Publications, 1991.
> A seminal work on the theology of ecological justice.

7. Byers, David M., ed. *Justice in the Marketplace: Collected Statements of the Vatican and U.S. Catholic Bishops on Economic Policy, 1891–1984.* Washington, D.C.: United States Catholic Conference, 1984.
> Collection of primary sources which deal with economic issues.

8. Calvez, J. Y., and Perrin, J. *The Church and Social Justice: The Social Teaching of the Popes from Leo XIII to Pius XII, 1878–1958.* Chicago: Regnery, 1961.
> Review of major themes of social teaching.

9. Coleman, John, S.J., ed. *One Hundred Years of Catholic Social Thought.* Maryknoll, N.Y.: Orbis Books, 1991.

An indispensable series of essays commemorating one hundred years of Catholic social teaching.

10. Cort, John C. *Christian Socialism.* Maryknoll, N.Y.: Orbis Books, 1988.

An in-depth historical treatment of the relationship between Christianity and socialism that explores the influence of Catholic social teaching on socialism.

11. Curran, Charles E., and McCormick, Richard A., S.J., eds. *Official Catholic Social Teaching: Readings in Moral Theology, No. 5.* New York: Paulist Press, 1986.

Excellent collection of essays tracing historical development, issues, and evaluations of the tradition of Catholic social teaching.

12. Curran, Charles E. *Catholic Social Teaching 1891–Present: A Historical, Theological and Ethical Analysis.* Washington, D.C.: Georgetown University Press, 2002.

A serious study of the methodology and content of Catholic social teaching with an emphasis on the historical development from the perspective of ethics and theology.

13. Donders, Joseph, ed. *John Paul II: The Encyclicals in Everyday Language.* Maryknoll, N.Y.: Orbis Books, 1995.

John Paul II's encyclicals in everyday language.

14. Dorr, Donal. *Option for the Poor: A Hundred Years of Vatican Social Teaching.* Maryknoll, N.Y.: Orbis Books, 1992.

Helpful analysis of each of the major papal and conciliar documents.

15. Dwyer, Judith, ed. *The New Dictionary of Catholic Social Thought.* Collegeville, Minn.: The Liturgical Press, 1994.

Provides analysis and commentary on the major social encyclicals and includes discussion of major movements, figures, themes and social issues in Catholic social thought.

16. Eagleson, John, and Scharper, Philip, eds. *Puebla and Beyond.* Trans. John Drury. Maryknoll, N.Y.: Orbis Books, 1979.

Complete texts from 1979 Puebla Conference of Latin American Bishops, plus very insightful commentaries.

17. Empereur, James L., S.J., and Kiesling, Christopher, O.P. *The Liturgy That Does Justice.* Collegeville, Minn.: The Liturgical Press, 1990.

The best development of the relationship between acting for justice and worshiping as a member of the Christian community.

18. Gremillion, Joseph, ed. *The Gospel of Peace and Justice: Catholic Social Teaching since Pope John.* Maryknoll, N.Y.: Orbis Books, 1975.

Collection of major documents of 1961–1974, with excellent introductory essay on themes and detailed index.

19. Himes, Kenneth R., O.F.M. and Himes, Michael. *Fullness of Faith: The Public Significance of Theology.* New York: Paulist Press, 1993.

Thoughtful, inspiring work providing theological reflection on Catholic social thought and public theology.

20. Himes, Kenneth R., O.F.M. *Responses to 101 Questions on Catholic Social Teaching.* Mahweh, N.J.: Paulist Press, 2001.

A readable question-and-answer format; an overview of major Catholic social teaching documents.

21. Hobgood, Mary E. *Catholic Social Teaching and Economic Theory.* Philadelphia: Temple University Press, 1991.

>A critical examination of economic paradigms which the author believes derive from Catholic social teaching.

22. Hollenbach, David. *Claims in Conflict-Retrieving and Renewing the Catholic Human Rights Tradition.* New York: Paulist Press, 1979.

>Thoughtful book on Catholic social teaching on human rights with its national and international themes.

23. Kammer, Fred C., S.J. *Doing Faithjustice: An Introduction to Catholic Social Thought.* Mahweh, N.J.: Paulist Press, 1994.

>A fresh perspective on the action necessary to implement Catholic social teaching.

24. Land, Philip S., S.J. *Shaping Welfare Consensus.* Washington, D.C.: Center of Concern, 1988.

>A provocative book that illustrates how the U.S. Catholic bishops have applied the principles of Catholic social teaching to the national discussion about public assistance programs.

25. Land, Philip S., S.J. *Catholic Social Teaching: As I Have Lived, Loathed and Loved It.* Chicago: Loyola University Press, 1994.

>A biographical and reflective book on the church adapting in a changing world with emphasis on labor, women, and differing cultures.

26. Mainelli, Vincent P. *Social Justice: The Catholic Position.* Washington, D.C.: Consortium Press, 1975.

>Documents from 1961–1974, with helpful index to major themes.

27. Massaro, Thomas, S.J. *Living Justice: Catholic Social Teaching in Action.* Franklin, Wis.: Sheed and Ward, 2000.

>Clearly written, concise synopses of Catholic social teaching with 9 key themes.

28. McKenna, Kevin E. *A Concise Guide to Catholic Social Teaching.* Notre Dame, Ind.: Ave Maria Press, 2002.

>Concise, user-friendly guide around seven social justice themes, with reflection questions.

29. Mich, Marvin L. *Catholic Social Teaching and Movements.* Mystic, Conn.: Twenty-Third Publications, 1998.

>This introduction to Catholic social teaching makes it alive and describes the movements and people who embodied the struggle for social justice.

30. Novak, Michael. *Freedom with Justice: Catholic Social Thought and Liberal Institutions.* San Francisco: Harper and Row, 1984.

>Critical review of the socially progressive trends in the Church's teaching by a prominent neo-conservative.

31. O'Brien, David J. and Shannon, Thomas A., eds. *Catholic Social Thought: The Documentary Heritage.* Maryknoll, N.Y.: Orbis Books, 1995.

>Comprehensive collection of major documents, including major pastoral letters of U.S. bishops.

32. Riley, Maria, O.P. *Transforming Feminism.* Kansas City, Mo.: Sheed and Ward, 1989.

>This book contains an interesting dialogue between feminism and Catholic social teaching.

33. Walsh, Michael and Davies, Brian, eds. *Proclaiming Justice and Peace: Papal Documents from* Rerum Novarum *through* Centesimus Annus. Mystic, Conn.: Twenty-Third Publications, 1991.

A compendium of official documents.